Praise for

THE DEEPLY FORMED LIFE

"*The Deeply Formed Life* is a book for our time. Honest, wise, insightful, funny, and—above all—deep. The way Rich and New Life Fellowship hold emotional health and racial justice together is beyond inspiring. This is spiritual formation for the future of the church."

—JOHN MARK COMER, pastor of teaching and vision at Bridgetown Church and author of *The Ruthless Elimination of Hurry*

"I've studied the Bible under Pastor Rich's leadership for close to a decade. The core values he shares in this book serve as guidance, not only for how we should live as Christians in an ever-changing world but also for how we can live a life of purpose—that consistently and enthusiastically points to Jesus."

—SUSAN KELECHI WATSON, actress from the award-winning television series *This Is Us*

"Rich Villodas masterfully integrates a wide range of sources—from contemplative to charismatic, monastic to missional, psychological to theological—in a way that is unmistakably Christ centered and gospel shaped. From his own deep spiritual journey, Rich has emerged with a voice that is warm and wise. His vulnerability is refreshing, and his distillation of these life-changing insights and practices is clear and compelling. I found myself smiling and feeling convicted by the Holy Spirit as I read it, and shouting, 'Amen.'"

—REV. DR. GLENN PACKIAM, associate senior pastor at New Life Church and author of *Blessed Broken Given*

"The evidence is everywhere—Christians have been formed by our culture for shallowness. The way to a more deeply formed life is no great mystery, but it is, as Rich Villodas shows, filled with countercultural practices that require intention, purpose, and vision. These pages cast a vision for not only deeper, holistic formation of each of us as individual believers but also for a more deeply formed church as well."

—KAREN SWALLOW PRIOR, author of
On Reading Well: Finding the Good Life Through Great Books and *Fierce Convictions: The Extraordinary Life of Hannah More—Poet, Reformer, Abolitionist*

"Rich Villodas writes from the wellspring of a monastic spirit that has been woven into the fabric of his life for years. I know very few Christian leaders who embody the contemplative life in such a way that connects the complex social, cultural, and spiritual realities we face today. *The Deeply Formed Life* invites us to journey with God toward personal wholeness and a new moral imagination that creates a better world of justice, peace, and reconciliation. I highly recommend it!"

—BRENDA SALTER MCNEIL, author of *Becoming Brave: Finding the Courage to Pursue Racial Justice Now*

"*The Deeply Formed Life* is a powerful call to a holy pursuit away from the temptations of a shallow discipleship that encumber our generation. Rich masterfully weaves the experiences and disciplines of both personal and communal formation that inspire and empower us to a contemporary discipleship, which leads to spiritual health

and flourishing. This book is a gift that enriches us as we open every layer."
—Rev. Dr. Gabriel Salguero, pastor at Calvario City Church and president of the National Latino Evangelical Coalition

"Rich Villodas understands that a pastor's primary task is not to gather a crowd but to form people in Christ. Spiritual formation is not a practice reserved for the spiritually elite; rather it is the very heart of all Christian discipleship. He embodies my hope for the contemporary church in the Western world—for us to a shift toward spiritual formation. *The Deeply Formed Life* clearly marks the path we need to follow, making the essential practices of formation accessible to everyone."
—Brian Zahnd, pastor of Word of Life Church in St. Joseph, Missouri, and author of *Sinners in the Hands of a Loving God*

"My friend Rich Villodas has been marked deeply by the spiritual directors of church history. And yet this book is not only about a call to engage in ancient practices so that we can have a more fulfilling life. Rich calls us to both personal refreshment *and* missional engagement, the kind of engagement that challenges injustice. I believe *The Deeply Formed Life* represents a new genre of spiritual direction, a kind modeled after Jesus, who both went away to pray and engaged the marginalized."
—Dr. Bryan Loritts, author of *The Dad Difference*

"*The Deeply Formed Life* tackles the endemic issue of non-discipleship within the Western church. The book is theologically rich, pastorally sensitive, and wonderfully practical. Rich does not shy away from addressing some of the most pressing issues in our day and how they affect our discipleship. This is much-needed!
—DEB HIRSCH, missional leader, speaker, and author of *Untamed: Reactivating a Missional Form of Discipleship* and *Redeeming Sex*

"In a captivating and moving way, which is profound and personal, Rich Villodas shows us how we can be formed by God into a masterpiece. With shimmering insights and poignant stories, this rare and powerful book will take you deeper into God and make the world more beautiful."
—KEN SHIGEMATSU, pastor of Tenth Church, Vancouver, BC, and bestselling author of *God in My Everything*

"Revealing our shallowness with grace and helping us see there is so much more to living, Rich Villodas leads us patiently into *The Deeply Formed Life*. Step by step, this pastor walks us through the malformations that plague our modern existence. He challenges us with content that has a personal spirituality and with nothing less than a full-orbed Christian discipleship. A powerful summons to the deeper life."
—DAVID FITCH, Lindner chair of evangelical theology at Northern Seminary Chicago and author of *Faithful Presence*

THE DEEPLY
FORMED LIFE

THE DEEPLY FORMED LIFE

Five Transformative Values
to Root Us in the
Way of Jesus

Foreword by Pete Scazzero

RICH VILLODAS

WATERBROOK

Details in some anecdotes and stories have been changed to protect the identities of the persons involved.

Library of Congress Cataloging-in-Publication Data
Names: Villodas, Rich, author.
Title: The deeply formed life : five transformative values to root us in the way of Jesus / Rich Villodas.
Description: First edition. | Colorado Springs, Colorado : WaterBrook, 2020.
Identifiers: LCCN 2020010606 | ISBN 9780525654384 (hardcover) | ISBN 9780525654391 (ebook)
Subjects: LCSH: Spiritual life—Christianity. | Christian life. | Spiritual formation.
Classification: LCC BV4501.3 .V55 2020 | DDC 248.4—dc23
LC record available at https://lccn.loc.gov/2020010606

Printed in Canada on acid-free paper

waterbrookmultnomah.com

1 2 3 4 5 6 7 8 9

First Edition

Book design by Elizabeth A. D. Eno

For Rosie.
Your love has deeply formed me.

FOREWORD

I never do this. Write forewords, I mean. On average, I turn down about one request per week to endorse books or write forewords. In fact, I even feel a little hesitant about this one, not because of the book (it's great, which I'll get to in a minute), but because I worry people will get the wrong idea and start asking me again and I'll stray from my God-given limits into a ministry that is not mine for this season.

But this book is worth breaking my rule to recommend. I love that it is, as Wendell Berry would say, *local*. It's grounded in a local church, where I hired Rich when he was just twenty-nine and where I've had the privilege to watch him grow, transition to become the lead pastor, and see him do great things for the congregation. This is important. Because Rich is fleshing these ideas out in *real* life, with *real* people. He's fleshing out ancient wisdom for this generation. He brings together both a rich breadth of reading, along with treasures discovered over time in the trenches of ministry. That's difficult. He's taken this to the next level, addressing vast resources of spiritual formation to the pressing issues of racial reconciliation, sexuality, and Sabbath rest. This is very significant and important as we transition into the third decade of the twenty-first century.

If you read this book, it will stretch you. It will challenge you to think more broadly about discipleship, especially how formation influences the most difficult opportunities of life today. You will find practical rhythms that will impact your life. And you might just find the life—the deep life—that you've been craving for a long time.

We can often ignore deeply intentional spiritual formation. Like our emotions, its roots lie hidden under the surface of our lives. But the invitation Rich extends here, to a life deeply formed by five pressing values, has the potential to transform us as individuals and as a culture. I find myself asking: *What would a family look like if its members lived with this kind of depth? How might singles? How about a neighborhood? A city? A nation?* It would transform life as we know it into something so much richer, so much more like what Jesus intended for his people.

So without further comment, I recommend this excellent book by a great man following Jesus and pastoring one of the most multiracial, diverse churches in a unique place called Queens in New York City.

Read on, and be formed.

—Pete Scazzero, founder of New Life Fellowship in New York and Emotionally Healthy Discipleship, and bestselling author of *Emotionally Healthy Spirituality* and *The Emotionally Healthy Leader*

CONTENTS

Foreword by Pete Scazzero vii

Introduction: Formed by a Shallow World xi

1 Contemplative Rhythms for an Exhausted Life 3

2 Deeply Formed Practices of Contemplative
Rhythms 20

3 Racial Reconciliation for a Divided World 43

4 Deeply Formed Practices of Racial Reconciliation ... 64

5 Interior Examination for a World Living
on the Surface 88

6 Deeply Formed Practices of Interior Examination ... 107

7 Sexual Wholeness for a Culture That
Splits Bodies from Souls 128

8 Deeply Formed Practices of Sexual Wholeness 148

9 Missional Presence in a Distracted and
Disengaged World 170

10 Deeply Formed Practices of Missional Presence ... 189

Afterword: The Deeply Formed Way Forward 215
Acknowledgments 221
Notes 223

INTRODUCTION:
FORMED BY A SHALLOW WORLD

Every now and then while I'm home sitting on the couch, I channel surf, looking for a good movie to watch. As is probably the case with you, there are some movies that, no matter how many times I've seen them, I'll watch again. They are on my running list, which contains such movies as *The Shawshank Redemption, The Lord of the Rings, The Godfather, Good Will Hunting,* and the romantic classic *Hitch,* just to name a few.

In addition to these, I'm a sucker for, well . . . *Titanic.* Who doesn't press rewind to see the baby-faced Jack (Leonardo DiCaprio) jigging with the sophisticated Rose (Kate Winslet) on the lower-deck dance floor? This blockbuster hit (the first movie to hit the billion-dollar mark)[1] featured a fancy necklace, Celine Dion hitting all the notes, and of course, a compelling story. But when I watched it recently, I was taken aback by a contrast I'd somehow missed before.

On the upper decks of the *Titanic,* there was amazing luxury—conspicuous opulence and riches. In stark contrast were the lower decks, where poverty-stricken passengers resided. Of course, a few days after the *Titanic* sailed, it struck an iceberg, and disaster was shared by all on board, no matter their socioeconomic status.

It was immediately after the tragic iceberg moment that I noticed another disturbing contrast. For those up on top, there was a tragic obliviousness. Everything still looked magnificent; life was great. But on the lower level, where the iceberg hit, it was a different story. Soon enough, the issues (the water) of the lower level began to rise to the upper deck. And in the final moments of the movie (spoiler alert!), the *Titanic* broke up and was consumed by the icy depths.

You can see the metaphor: sooner or later the issues on life's lower decks, though we remain oblivious, will nevertheless rise to the top. Truthfully, there are many with us (in our families, churches, schools, and workplaces) who are in the same boat, all unwittingly in danger of being broken up and sucked down. In fact, it often can feel as though our entire world is going under.

Pushing the metaphor a bit further, on the upper decks of our social media lives, things can also look great—impressive, even. (At least our Instagram gives that impression.) We like to put ourselves forward as competent, capable people. But as a pastor, I've repeatedly seen the truth behind the images we carefully curate.

I routinely meet with people who, when I get up close, present a picture that's not reflected on social media. From time to time, I actually go back to their profiles to look at some of their photos (sounds a bit stalkerish, I know). I scroll for one purpose only: to be reminded that very often, things are not as they appear. Topside, people can look so content, joyful, and successful, but privately beneath they'll confess suicidal thoughts, drug addictions, marital affairs, debilitating shame, inner rage, and so much more—I see the icy waters rising. It's a wake-up call. When I look at my own social media profile, I know that from my own depths, similarly threatening waters can be rising.

> We won't take time to go deep down within because we have often been discipled into superficiality.

Actually, it is in those very lower decks where our spiritual lives take true shape and texture. But notoriously, we won't take time to go deep down within because we have often been discipled into superficiality—and in the name of Jesus, no less. This superficiality works against us as we try to navigate some of the most complex issues of our world, whether related to our emotional health or the complexities of race, sexuality, and justice.

How are we to experience wholeness in our own personal lives while being instruments of healing in a world that is breaking apart around us? To start, we must live in a different place. We have to go down to the lower decks.

At New Life Fellowship, the church I pastor, we decided to use the iceberg as our logo. But in our usage, it's not a device of destruction but a symbol pointing us to depth of transformation.

The iceberg brings to mind the goal of spiritual formation in Christ—namely, that Jesus wants to form his life in us. Significantly, about 90 percent of an iceberg remains unseen beneath the surface.² And Jesus wants to transform our entire beings, not just the 10 percent that shows. Yet Christianity in the Western world is often marginalized as a life accessory rather than the means of powerful life transformation. Still, the emphasis upon surface change is ubiquitous within Christianity and finds expression across all traditions, denominations, and movements.

I thank God that for more than twenty years, I've spent time in a variety of Christian traditions that seek him and offer great gifts to the world. Yet I've also witnessed a kind of dichotomizing of faith where the emphasis is on the outward at the expense of the inward. For instance:

- In some conservative traditions, transformation is about getting the right theology in one's head while overlooking the inner work God wants to do.

- In some progressive traditions, transformation is about right action and engagement within the world but often at the expense of personal humility and mercy.

- In some Charismatic and Pentecostal traditions, transformation is about getting the right experience but without the deeper work of loving well and exploring our inner worlds.

At New Life, we've discovered time and time again, for more than three decades, that the work God wants to do in us requires us to look within: to look deeper and be deeply formed. Why? Because we are covertly and consistently being formed by a culture fashioned by shallowness. In short, we are being shallowly formed.

WE ARE ALWAYS BEING (SHALLOWLY) FORMED

Whether we know it or not, see it or not, or understand it or not, we are always at risk of being shallowly formed. We are formed by our false selves, our families of origin, the highly manipulated presentations of social media, and the value system of a world that determines worth based on accomplishments, possessions, efficiency, intellectual acumen, and gifts. So we need to be regularly called back to the essence of our lives in God. That essence is one of ongoing transformation; that is, Christ being formed in us. It's something I've needed to continually explore during all my years of following Jesus.

I vividly remember words spoken to me in my early twenties by a college professor at the end of a class on leadership, three years after I'd become a follower of Jesus. I had the task of reading a book on postmodernism and the church and presenting my findings to the class. Problem was, I didn't read the book.

Sure, I had done my own study of postmodernism: skimming the dustcover and chapter outline of the book. And then I gave my own presentation of the topic. Halfway through, the professor stopped me midsentence and said, "Rich, you haven't read the book, right?"

I sheepishly responded, "No, I haven't," and heard the snickers and whispers of my classmates. I had ten more minutes left to go in my presentation. I thought I would be asked to sit.

Instead, he said, "Keep going."

At the end of the class, the professor asked if he could have a word with me. As I stood in front of him with one strap of my book bag hanging over my shoulder, in no uncertain terms he spoke a word of warning to me: "Rich, you have a gift for reading the dustcover of a book and being able to give a thirty-minute presentation on it. But you also have a curse. The curse is, you will be tempted to believe that you can live your life off your gifts and not do the deep work of character formation. Your gifts can take you only so far. But there are no such limits when it comes to a life marked by deep character."

Those words pierced my heart. To be sure, I resented him for a few days. The nerve of him to say that I had a curse. But that moment was a turning point for me, even at the young age of twenty-two. I was learning about being deeply formed.

UNTIL CHRIST IS FORMED IN YOU

In one of his letters, the apostle Paul named the painful and astonishing desire he had for a body of Christ followers in Galatia (in modern-day Turkey). He wrote to a group of people marked by a preoccupation with religious changes that kept them from experiencing deep transformation in Christ. How Paul's letter began makes it clear how shocked he was by their way of life. A few verses into the letter, Paul wrote, "I am astonished that you are so quickly deserting him who called you in the grace of Christ and are turning to a different gospel—not that there is another one, but there are some who trouble you and want to distort the gospel of Christ" (Galatians 1:6–7).

The Galatians had drifted away from the simple message of God's grace found in the Christ that Paul preached. Certainly, this message (the gospel) had begun to transform them. Soon after, however, certain teachers started infiltrating the church, teaching another gospel. This other gospel was cosmetic.

The false teachers in that church basically said that faith in Jesus was not enough. If you were a man, in order to be accepted as part of the people of God, you needed to be circumcised, you had to observe specific holy days, and you especially had to maintain the customs of Jewish religious culture. In essence, they were saying, "If you believe in Jesus and do these things, you will be the people of God. If you do this, you will be the covenant people. If you do this, you will prove yourself to have been properly 'formed.'"

What use are the superficial changes we make if we neglect the deep work God wants to do inside us?

But Paul spoke an unequivocal *no!* We are not transformed from the outside in; we are transformed from the inside out. One is transformed by saying yes again and again to Christ's self-giving, poured-out, redemptive love. We receive it and are to be formed by it. This was Paul's fixation. He later in this same letter described his concern for his "little children" by saying, "I am again in the anguish of childbirth until Christ is formed in you!" (4:19).

Paul had one solitary focus: that Christ be formed in them. What use are the superficial changes we make if we neglect the deep work God wants to do inside us? Although Paul was writing to a church two thousand years ago, this issue they were facing is the very same in our day. Instead of being deeply formed, we settle for being shallowly shaped.

MY STORY OF BEING FORMED

I'm a New Yorker of Puerto Rican descent, born and raised in the East New York section of Brooklyn. In the 1980s and '90s, this area of Brooklyn was regarded as one of the most overlooked, under-resourced, drug-infested areas in New York City. Growing up in this neighborhood offered me a mixed bag of experiences. I have fond memories of playing street football and frightening memories of seeing a couple of dead bodies in the street.

I have stories of profoundly joyful moments playing with more than a dozen cousins who lived down the block from me and heart-wrenching stories of relatives dying prematurely because of drug use and violence. I have grown up with wonderful examples of men and women of faith around me (some who were my grandparents and aunts), as well as examples of familial dysfunction. All of these experiences have formed me.

I grew up in a home that was indifferent to the things

of faith. I didn't have many negative views about the church or God. I rarely thought of them. During my childhood, my parents attended church once a year at best, but they made up for their indifference by regularly sending me to church with my grandparents. At first, I thought my parents wanted to instill in me good religious values and such, but I would come to find out that these trips to church gave Mom and Dad a much-needed break. (Those two especially lacked religious curiosity if it meant sitting through four hours of a Pentecostal church service spoken in Spanish.)

This church I attended shaped my first conceptions of God. As early as elementary-school age, I learned that God was unpredictable and powerful. At any moment, someone in the congregation could be the meeting place where the holy converged with the human. As a kid, I curiously and fearfully watched people fall on the ground, dance, shout, and cry. When this happened, there was both a normalcy and sacredness that filled the congregation. It was all a bit too much for me to absorb, but I was intrigued.

I would also learn that God was in the business of healing and welcoming. I recall moments when drug addicts would come into a church service (usually attended by twenty people) to make their presence known. One person who walked in often was an inebriated uncle of mine, and in the process of his grand, disruptive entrance, he would be met by a couple of deacons who would welcome him, pray for him, and winsomely escort him out if needed. I would see from an early age that the house of God was a sacred place for hospitality and a safe place for the hurting.

As a twelve-year-old, I asked my parents if I could stop going to church, and they obliged. But five years later, I found myself back in church as a senior in high school. I had started to date a pastor's daughter. (That got me back into the church enthusiastically.) The relationship lasted a couple of years, and when it ended, I was sent into a tailspin of anxiety and depression. I needed some kind of peace in my life, so on one August Sunday night, I returned to the church I'd visited as a child. In that moment, I encountered the love of God in a way that broke through my despair.

I walked into the church, which had about one hundred people in attendance. It was a long, narrow storefront building filled to capacity. After the loud and boisterous time of singing, I listened to a former drug-addict-turned-preacher give a sermon from Ezekiel 37, a story about God breathing life into a valley of dry bones (see verses 1–14). As he preached (in English and Spanish without a translator), he paced back and forth, sometimes dancing up and down the center aisle, with fancy brown alligator shoes and a matching belt.

At the close of his sermon, he invited all who wanted "the breath of God" (see verses 5–6) to come forward for prayer. I knew I was spiritually and emotionally suffocating and took him up on the offer. My soul was like that valley of dry bones, and I longed for God's life, so I went forward. As the preacher prayed for me, with sweat dripping down his forehead and tears flowing down my face, I became that meeting place where the holy converged with the human. I (along with about fifteen of my family members) received the gracious invitation to life in Christ.

From this point on, something was unlocked in me. I found myself praying all the time. I attended every church service and Bible study my local congregation offered. I would be in church five to six days out of the week, participating in the prayer meeting, youth group, and men's ministry—even the weekly women's Bible study. I invited myself into every home prayer group I could find. When I wasn't at a church meeting, I was sitting shoulder to shoulder with my grandfather in his bedroom, being mentored in the Scriptures. It was hard to explain what was happening, but I had found something for which my soul was thirsting.

That was the beginning of my continuing spiritual journey forward. Along the path, I would be exposed to many different ways of following Jesus. As a twenty-one-year-old college student, I would be exposed to the desert fathers and mothers and would begin experimenting with practices of silence, solitude, and contemplation. As a twenty-three-year-old, I would learn more about how God transformed people through the presence and ministry of the Holy Spirit. As a twenty-five-year-old, I would come to know of God's particular and preferential care for the poor. I learned with great clarity that the spiritually, emotionally, *and* socially poor mattered to God and should matter to me. As a twenty-eight-year-old, I would begin a journey of interior examination, integrating the world of my feelings and emotions into my spiritual formation. As a thirty-year-old, I would be introduced to the radical vision of God's reconciling power across racial, cultural, economic, and gender barriers.

Throughout this book, I will share the stories, insights, and failures that have marked my journey. I've been shaped by shoutin' churches and silent experiences. I've sung Taizé and memorized Black gospel songs. I've prayed at 3:00 a.m. with Trappist monks to start the day and at 3:00 a.m. with Pentecostals to close the night. I've been enamored with liturgy and slain in the Spirit. I've preached on justification by faith and faith that leads to justice in our world.

For more than twenty years as a follower of Jesus, I have been privileged to be shaped by a wide assortment of streams and traditions, and I've learned that to be deeply formed requires one to be widely informed—not on a cognitive level alone but also in a way that the very makeup of our lives is profoundly shaped. I have discovered repeatedly that faithful Christian witness requires us to hold on to the beautiful and diverse manifestations of God's action among his people, stretching ourselves to be more faithful than ever to Jesus and his kingdom in the age in which we live. The best way I can illustrate this is through the example of redwood trees.

A POWERFUL ROOT SYSTEM

On a recent speaking trip to the San Francisco area, my family and I spent a weekend at a camp that was surrounded by what seemed like an endless number of redwood trees. When we first encountered these majestic trees on our drive to the camp, I gasped in wonder and amazement. I'm a city guy. I'm used to tall buildings and crowded streets. But seeing these tall trees crammed together like New York City subway riders during rush hour opened up something in my soul.

After settling in our cottage, we walked around the campgrounds. For fifteen minutes, I walked with my head craned upward, contemplating these trees that were as tall as two hundred feet. I would learn that some redwood trees grow up to almost four hundred feet, similar to a thirty-seven-story building. It was almost too much for me to take in.

What I learned about redwood trees that weekend would give me a vision for this book. As I waited to preach one of the sessions, a pastor named Will from the church that hosted us stepped onto the stage to lead the congregation in prayer. Will also was of Puerto Rican descent, with long thick dreadlocks that reminded me of the redwood trees.

He offered some words about community life and gave a short lesson on the root system of the redwoods, informing us that these redwood trees are centered and strong because their roots are robustly intertwined with each other. The roots often go only five or six feet deep, but they extend outward up to a hundred feet from the trunk. Each tree is deeply sustained by the larger, wider system of roots that provides stability, enabling them to grow high into the sky.

As I learned this new information and studied redwood trees further, I came to the realization that a redwood tree is the core metaphor for Christian spiritual formation that we need in our day. God longs for us to be fully alive, soaring into the sky and bearing witness to God's good life that is available to us. But if we hope to be shaped and changed in this way of life, we must have a root system powerful enough to hold us together.

What I want to propose is that there is a root system

from which our lives and surrounding world would greatly benefit. A deeply formed life is a life marked by integration, intersection, intertwining, and interweaving, holding together multiple layers of spiritual formation. This kind of life calls us to be people who cultivate lives with God in prayer, move toward reconciliation, work for justice, have healthy inner lives, and see our bodies and sexuality as gifts to steward.

> A deeply formed life is marked by integration, holding together multiple layers of spiritual formation.

Although this might sound like an impossible standard, I believe that by God's grace, the presence of the Spirit, and the support of the body of Christ, we can all intentionally and incrementally move to a more comprehensive view and practice of life in Christ. What I propose as the goal of this book is not a quick-fix strategy to solve all our problems but rather a long-term vision to help us have greater depth and maturity as we engage our problems.

THE DEEPLY FORMED LIFE

In this book, I will explore five values in which we need to be deeply formed. I recognize that this is not all there is to engage, but these are five areas that nonetheless need to be held together. As we seek to follow Jesus, we need to harness a multilayered approach of Christian identity and mission. We do need these.

1. *Contemplative rhythms for an exhausted life.* Most of us live at a nonstop outward pace, which leaves no time to be with God and actually does violence against our souls. As one who has been shaped by the ancient desert and monastic traditions, I see the riches and resources available to root us in a way of life that is slow, vibrant, and transformative. I will offer a vision for a life that isn't consumed by the hurried and harried ways of the world.

2. *Racial reconciliation for a divided world.* Because the church I pastor has people from at least seventy-five nations, the hostility of our world has often come right into our community. We have journeyed more than three decades together, offering a way forward as a prophetic community in a deeply partisan and ideologically segregated culture. I will present a pathway of reconciliation for us to take together.

3. *Interior examination for a world living on the surface.* Many of us lack the tools to effectively navigate our interior worlds. Our unawareness cripples us with anxiety, and we miss opportunities to grow into mature people who love well. I will serve as a tour guide for helping us explore the notoriously uncharted waters of our inner worlds.

4. *Sexual wholeness for a culture that splits bodies from souls.* We often don't know what a healthy integra-

tion of our spiritual lives and our bodies looks like. We will explore the process of loving God with our whole selves and seeing our bodies as gifts to steward for the flourishing of our own lives and relationships.

5. *Missional presence for a distracted and disengaged people.* What does it mean to make space in our lives for others? How do we engage the troubling realities of injustice, poverty, and spiritually struggling people? Studying this theme will help us move out into the world to be a presence of healing and hope for others.

Each of these five values will have two corresponding chapters. The first offers theological and biblical vision to help us see the big picture, and the second offers simple (yet not easy) practices that can position us on the deeply formed journey.

A WORD ABOUT THE PRACTICES

The deeply formed life is not possible without an intentional reordering of our lives. This is why you'll find many different ways to flesh out the content of this book in the real world. However, before we consider them, I need to offer a few words about the practices themselves.

First, the practices don't save us or make God love us more. We are saved by God's free and faithful love in Christ. God's love is steadfast, meaning there's nothing we can do to make him love us more, and there's nothing we can do to make him love us less. Rather, these practices are meant to help us receive and express God's love in deeply formed ways.

The practices have personal and communal elements to them. Some practices don't require the involvement of other people, but each practice is strengthened by the presence of others on the journey. The practices are best held together in a community where we are surrounded by different people who powerfully bear witness to an area of formation in which we might not be so strong. We are all, in some area of our lives, like the paralyzed man in the Gospels (see Mark 2:1–12). From time to time, we need friends who have the strength to bring us before Jesus.

The practices are meant to complement and enliven such core spiritual practices as Sunday worship, receiving the sacraments, hearing the gospel preached, and gathering with others for prayer and friendship. Practices are not just about what we do; they're also a means of reframing how we think and see.

The practices take time. It's called practice because we can always learn something new. There might be some practices that you begin to implement quickly and, in the process, you experience significant fruit. There might be practices that take a long time to get a handle on. Give yourself the same grace God has granted you.

MY PASTORAL CONTEXT

I have the great privilege of pastoring New Life Fellowship Church in Queens, New York City. We are a multiracial, urban, multiclass, immigrant, ethnically diverse, multigenerational community of people trying to love Jesus and each other well. We live in the city that never sleeps and have the same struggles of every city dweller. I note this because most books about spiritual formation are often written with mountains, the woods, and monasteries pristinely positioned in the background. I write, think, and live with the background of sirens blaring, homeless men pouring into our church building for showers, and neighbors frantically running to catch the subway. The deeply formed life is not simply for people who have the benefit of environments conducive to silence and solitude. From personal experience, I can assure you that it's for people of all walks of life who long to be shaped by God's gracious love. My hope is that in these pages, God will invite you into a profound encounter of that same love.

This brings me to our first area of focus: living with contemplative rhythms.

THE DEEPLY
FORMED LIFE

ONE

Contemplative Rhythms
for an Exhausted Life

In 1901, an American doctor named John Harvey Girdner coined the term *Newyorkitis* to describe an illness that
had symptoms including edginess, quick movements, and
impulsiveness. At the time, he said it was "a disease which
affects a large percentage of the inhabitants of Manhattan
Island."[1] As a native New Yorker, I can't help but laugh
and also gasp at these words. I laugh because Girdner is
describing a world long gone: a world without the internet, high-speed cars, and other technological advances
that inform everything we do. I gasp, however, because if
Newyorkitis is what Girdner observed more than one hundred years ago, where does that leave us today?

Girdner saw something in 1901 that captured the
dangerous pace at which we often unwittingly live. Our
world hasn't slowed down. Our world continues on,
faster and busier, and we are reminded that our souls
were not created for the kind of speed to which we have
grown accustomed. Thus, we are a people who are out of
rhythm, a people with too much to do and not enough

time to do it. This illness is no longer a New York phe-
nomenon—it has infected people around the world. And
I see it every day.

Recently on a Saturday morning, I was walking through
my neighborhood, and as I neared my apartment building, an older man frantically shouted across the street,
"Are you Jewish?" He waved his hands at me as if he had
been stranded on a deserted island and I was his ticket
back to civilization. He repeated again as he drew closer,
"Are you Jewish?" This was a strange question, but it oc-
curred to me I had been growing out my beard, so that
might explain the question.

I responded a bit too loudly for an early Saturday
morning, "No, I'm Puerto Rican."

"Okay, great," he said as he tried to catch his breath,
wiping sweat from his forehead. "I need your help. I have
to get my ninety-year-old mother downstairs."

It was a slow morning for me, so with curiosity I followed him into his apartment building. When we got to
the elevator, he pointed at the buttons while distractedly
looking in the other direction. "Press six, please," he
said—another strange moment, but I willingly did so.
On the ride up, we exchanged names and then awkwardly
stared at the numbers. His breathing was heavy and la-
bored. I looked at him from the corner of my eye to see
him talking under his breath.

We took the elevator up six stories. Then, as he was
about to step into his small apartment, he shouted, "Ma,
Rich is here."

His mother shouted back with irritation, "Who's
Rich?" (This was quite a New York moment.)

I stepped in and saw a frail, well-dressed elderly woman

grasping her walker. She had on a large pearl necklace and heels that looked a bit too big for her. With exasperation, she grumbled things like, "I'm so busy," "There's never enough time," and "How am I going to finish everything?"

Soon I found out that this mom-and-son duo were heading to the local synagogue but that he couldn't press the elevator button due to Sabbath prohibitions. All he wanted me to do was press the elevator button—nothing more, nothing less.

I look back at that moment and chuckle. But what struck me most in this whole encounter was that this elderly woman was stressed out because of the fullness of her life. Here she was, overwhelmed, on the Sabbath of all days, with too much to do at ninety years of age.

Newyorkitis is alive and well.

DANGEROUSLY DEPLETED

Our lives can easily take us to the brink of burnout. The pace we live at is often destructive. The lack of margin is debilitating. We are worn out. In all of this, the problem before us is not just the frenetic pace we live at but what gets pushed out from our lives as a result; that is, *life with God*. Educator and activist Parker Palmer makes a compelling case that burnout typically does not come about because we've given so much of ourselves that we have nothing left. He tells us, "It merely reveals the nothingness from which I was trying to give in the first place."[2]

What would it look like to live at a different pace? What if there were a rhythm of life that could instead enable us to deeply connect with God, a lifestyle not dominated by hurry and exhaustion but by margin and joy? As long as we remain enslaved to a culture of speed, superficiality, and distraction, we will not be the people God longs for us to be. We desperately need a spirituality that roots us in a different way.

> As long as we remain enslaved to a culture of speed, superficiality, and distraction, we will not be the people God longs for us to be.

No matter our walks of life or professions, our struggle is all too real: single parents trying to find just a moment of oasis from the incessant bickering of children, doctors caught in the unending pressures of life-and-death choices, and pastors over-functioning to the point of breakdown. There are schoolteachers whose work never really ends, sleep-deprived students floundering through exams, immigrant small-business owners struggling to make ends meet, and therapists and social workers overwhelmed with the bottomless crises they need to resolve daily. The pace of our lives can be brutal.

Without denying these realities, we are invited to a different way of being in the world. The late Japanese theologian Kosuke Koyama wrote a book titled *Three-Mile-an-Hour God*.[3] Dr. Koyama was trying to convey that if we want to connect with God, we'd be wise to travel at God's speed. God has all the time in the world, and as a result he is not in a rush. Thus, Koyama's claim that God travels at three miles an hour is not an arbitrary figure. On average, humans walk at this pace. And it's in just such ambling, unhurried, and leisurely moments that we often encounter God. N. T. Wright similarly affirmed, "It is only when we slow down our lives that we can catch up to God."[4] This is the paradox of contemplative rhythms.

Now, don't get me wrong; I'm not advocating that we go back to dial-up internet service and take boats instead of airplanes to our destinations. Speed has helped remake our world in ways that are wonderful and liberating. But speed has also caused our connections with God and others to be incredibly superficial. There's a severe lack of depth in our lives and communities because we have allowed ourselves to be swept up by a world under the influence of addictive speed. And as philosopher Dallas Willard famously said, "Hurry is the great enemy of spiritual life in our day."[5]

In the face of this crisis of speed, distraction, and superficial spirituality, there is a way that has been tried and tested through the centuries. It's a way that has marked my life from the time I became a Christian as a young adult. It's the way of the monastic, contemplative life. We live in a time when we must learn from the monastery. We desperately need a way of thinking and living that isn't captive to the powers of efficiency, speed, and performance. We need a way of living according to a different understanding of time and space. We need the treasures of monastic imagination.

A MONASTIC IMAGINATION

Before you dismiss this notion as an old, irrelevant idea from the Dark Ages, let me attempt to reveal the monastic approach as an important correction to our way of life and faith. As pastor Ken Shigematsu stated, "Every one of us has a monk or nun 'embryo' inside of us."[6] Deep in our souls, we crave space with God that is defined by silence, stillness, and solitude.

My first experience of this kind of monastic spirituality was in college, and it forever changed me. As a student at Nyack College in Rockland County, New York, I was required to take a personal spiritual-formation class my senior year. Part of the class was to go on a weekend retreat at a Franciscan monastery. During the weekend, the students were placed in different parts of the grounds for about eight hours to just "be with God." In my case, I was told to remain on the platform of an outdoor chapel, with no Bible, only a journal. My assignment was to remain in solitude and write about the experience. This was one of the most challenging and exhilarating days of my life.

I would close my eyes and listen to the beautiful sounds of birds chirping and then in the next moment stare into the ground and see a colony of ants working diligently. In the stillness of the moment, every part of creation somehow connected me to God.

I'd look out into the empty rows of wooden chairs, wondering about my future life of preaching. I'd fix my gaze on the statue of baby Jesus being tenderly held by Joseph at the center of the platform. As I closed my eyes and took deep breaths, I imagined God holding me in that tender embrace. There were moments of delightful contemplation when I heard words of God's grace spoken deep within my heart. I journaled many pages of prayers, fears, and requests, and when I got tired of writing, I just stared out into the monastery grounds.

Now, I don't want you to get the idea that it was all heavenly; it wasn't. There were also times of sheer boredom and dread, when I was disinterested and wanted to be somewhere else. I mean, after just an hour of solitude and silence, I was ready to go home. But I was stuck there. To break up the monotony, I'd jog in place, do push-ups, and (not sure I should confess this) take power naps on the sturdy Eucharist table.

Yet something happened in me that day. From that moment, the appetite of my soul was awakened. Upon returning to my college campus, I found myself sneaking off to the library or to quiet spaces to pray, as if I were doing something illicit. Something was planted in me, and I knew I needed to follow this path more intentionally.

Some five years later, I joined the New Life Fellowship pastoral staff. I was reintroduced to the riches of monasticism, as this church had been drawing from this tradition for a long time. In my years on staff, I have had the privilege of spending many hours in prayer at monasteries and in study with monks. What I've learned has reinforced the truth that unless we live with an intentional commitment to slow down, we have no hope for a quality of life that allows Jesus to form us into his image.

Monastic spirituality means slowing our lives down to be with God. In a world that operates at a frenetic pace and with the addiction of achievement, slowing down brings us to a place of centeredness and stillness before God. It gives us the opportunity to be present to God throughout the day.

PRACTICING THE PRESENCE OF GOD

This concept of being present to God throughout the day was popularized by a man named Brother Lawrence. Brother Lawrence was a seventeenth-century Carmelite monk who wrote a famous book called *The Practice of the Presence of God*. The concept of the book is straightforward. In every activity in which you are engaged, remember that God is present and offer your heart to him in prayer. If you're washing the dishes, writing a paper, or watching the Mets play (Lord, please help my Mets), we are to be present to God. Simple enough, right? Well, in my life and in the lives of people I have spoken to about this, being present to God is one of the most difficult things to do.

As I reflected on Brother Lawrence's life, it struck me that I sometimes forget that he lived in a unique setting. His ability to "practice the presence of God," difficult as it might have been, was still more attainable because of the structure and rhythm of his life. When followers of Jesus try to implement the practice of the presence of God in the way of Brother Lawrence, without the structure and rhythm of his life, it can easily lead to perpetual disappointment and disconnection.

The problem, as I see it, is that we forget he lived in a monastery, which ought to give us some insight (and relief) into his life situation. There were fixed hours of prayer he observed. He prayed in community and in solitude. His entire life was ordered in a way that was conducive to communion with God. Now you might be thinking, *That's fine, but I don't live in a monastery.* Neither do I. Nevertheless, I have discovered that any effort given to ordering my life around rhythms of silence, solitude, and prayer has significantly enriched my life.

For many Christians, the word *monastic* carries cultural baggage and theological misunderstandings. Consequently, far too many people dismiss the gifts and culture offered by this tradition. As we consider the historical and biblical aspects of monasticism, hopefully we will be open to applying this approach to our full and busy lives.

MONASTIC MOMENTS IN SCRIPTURE

The monastic life is rooted in the pages of Scripture. The word *monk* comes from the Greek word *monachos,* which means "solitary." Monastic life is ordered by a value and urgency to be united with God in prayer. Although there is much more to monastic life (such as vows of poverty and celibacy), I'd like to highlight the monastic distinctives of prayer, silence, and solitude.

When searching for theological grounds for monastic practice, I found that the Bible is replete with examples of people who lived a life shaped by solitude, silence, and a slowed-down spirituality. Let me offer brief sketches of Moses, David, Mary, John the Baptist, and Jesus.

Moses: a man of the desert. While early on he had been molded in the ways of Egypt, he was gripped by the oppression of the Jewish people and tragically took matters into his own hands. In a moment of justice-fueled anger, he murdered an Egyptian and fled into the desert.

During his forty years in this place, he lived an existence marked by silence and solitude. Think for a moment of what it might have been like for Moses on a given day: no Wi-Fi, no car, and no crowds. Every day, Moses dwelled for hours in silence while watching over his flocks.

We don't have anything in Scripture that gives detail to his spiritual practices, but it's not a coincidence that God chose to reveal himself to Moses in the silent context of a burning bush.

David: a man after God's own heart who was shaped in monasticism. Much of the psalms that David wrote sprouted from a place of silence and solitude. David was a man of contemplation, a man of silence. In one psalm, he wrote, "One thing have I asked of the LORD, that will I seek after: that I may dwell in the house of the LORD all the days of my life, to gaze upon the beauty of the LORD and to inquire in his temple" (27:4).

David's life as a young man was one of stillness. Certainly, his younger years were also marked by sheepshearing, songwriting, and fighting giants, lions, and bears. But even in the chaos and unpredictable life he lived, he guarded the stillness to prioritize God's presence.

The songs he wrote and music he played flowed from a context of monastic rhythm. David wrote psalms about quieting his soul (see 131:2), making his soul "wait in silence" (62:5), and being still and knowing that God is God (see 46:10). Psalms is the prayer book of the Bible, and it is one that emerges from the depths of contemplation and reflection.

Mary: a young woman formed by contemplative pondering and deep reflection. When the angel Gabriel offered her good news from God, Mary "treasured up all these things, pondering them in her heart" (Luke 2:19).

Mary was one who beheld the Lord in stillness and

solitude. She listened to the Word of God carefully and intently, allowing herself to be formed by it. She entered into meditation, pondering the sheer absurdity of the angel's message and marveling at the astonishing invitation therein. She was one given to depth of thought, opening her entire being—physically and spiritually—to the God who graciously came.

John the Baptist: a solitary prophet who spent much of his life in the wilderness. He was a man given to prayer, solitude, and silence (and some strange eating habits). John cultivated life with God in the wilderness, and it was out of that place that he offered prophetic and powerful words of God's heart to prepare the way of the Lord for a people who had gone astray.

Jesus: Son of God, Son of Man—he cannot be truthfully understood apart from his deep commitment to a monastic kind of life. Jesus was regularly active in preaching, healing, casting out demons, and far more, but his life would be self-contradicting apart from the long hours spent with the Father in silence and solitude. One could make a strong case that the fully human Jesus was able to live the life he did because of the constant time and energy put into being with the Father in prayer.

In the gospel of Luke, after Jesus was baptized, the voice of the Father broke through the sky, and Jesus received a word of affirmation: "You are my beloved Son; with you I am well pleased" (3:22). Immediately following this scene, Jesus spent forty days in the wilderness being tempted by the Evil One. Alone and in the setting of the desert, Jesus encountered Satan and refused to be identified by anything other than the affirmation of the Father.

It was after this grueling battle that Jesus returned to

civilization and recited, "The Spirit of the Lord is upon me, because he has anointed me" (4:18). Over and over in the Gospels, Jesus conveys the power of God, and then he returns to be in communion with the God from whom that power flows.

MONASTICISM IN THE EARLY CENTURIES

Beyond the testimony of Scripture, monastic spirituality has marked the story of the early Christian church. In the first and second century after the resurrection of Jesus, men and women would flee to the desert to be with God for a variety of reasons. The early desert fathers and mothers were people who felt a strong call to prayer, solitude, silence, fasting, and other spiritual disciplines. It's hard to truly know who was the first to establish this way of following Jesus, but for our purposes here, one of the most noteworthy explanations of the remarkable surge of monasticism came as a result of Christian faith losing its distinctiveness and radical call.

For the first few centuries, Christianity was a marginalized and persecuted religion. The book of Acts describes the resistance and cost one experienced for being a follower of Jesus and claiming him Lord of the world. Despite the unrelenting danger of confessing Jesus as God and King, Christianity spread like wildfire.

Christians were people on the edges of society, proclaiming the radical message of the kingdom of God, serving the poor, healing the sick, and subverting the way of the empire. But something shifted in the cultural landscape in the fourth century, leaving devout Christians with an important decision on how they would live.

On the eve of a battle in the early part of the century, Constantine (who would become emperor of Rome) claimed to have had a revelation. In the revelation, Constantine said he was instructed to place a Christian symbol on the shields of his soldiers. Church historian Justo González explained: "Constantine ordered that his soldiers should use on their shield and on their standard or *labarum* a symbol that looked like the superimposition of the Greek letters chi and rho. Since these are the first two letters of the name, 'Christ,' this *labarum* could well have been a Christian symbol."[7]

Having done so, Constantine achieved victory over his enemies and in turn transformed the way the empire related to Christians. In a sweeping turn of events, Christianity went from persecuted religion to friend of the empire. In light of this significant shift, new questions on faith and discipleship arose.

For many Christians, a different kind of crisis of faith surfaced. González further wrote, "The narrow gate of which Jesus had spoken had become so wide that countless multitudes were hurrying through it—many seeming to do so only in pursuit of privilege and position, without caring to delve too deeply into the meaning of Christian baptism and life under the cross."[8] In other words, Christianity had experienced a drastic cultural shift whereby people purported to enter into life with God and the church not by renunciation of the ways of the world system but by appropriating it through political and cultural power.

It was in this context that men and women decided to

take up their cross and go into the desert. No longer was there a significant price to pay to follow Jesus. No longer was there a clear and powerful delineation between Christianity and conformity to the political ways of the world. In order to resist the temptations of worldly power, men and women went into the desert to maintain a cross-shaped life that would be marked by prayer, renunciation, and formative spiritual practices.

The genesis of monastic life in a post-Constantine world in the fourth century serves as a powerful reminder for us today. In short, the way of worldly power, values, and priorities can easily take precedence in our lives, with Christianity being either complicit in the perpetuation of the world system or irrelevant in the social landscape.

The desert fathers, mothers, and later monastics remind us that the way of following Jesus requires a steadfast refusal to get caught up in the pace, power, and priorities of the world around us. We are called to have our lives shaped by a different kind of power, pace, and priorities, offered to us by God.

LEAVING THE WORLD

In the same way of these early monastics, we are invited to leave the world, along with its enticements and false messages of assurance. The deeply formed life is one that takes seriously the call of renunciation. We are regularly being formed by the pace, noise, and values of the surrounding world. Yet to be deeply formed is to regularly come back to a different rhythm—a rhythm marked by communion, reflection, and a life-giving pace that enables us to offer our presence to the present moment. But living at this pace means we need to leave the world. This is the paradox of following Jesus. It's only when we leave the world that we can truly be at home in it.

Theologian and poet Thomas Merton once wrote, "Solitude is to be preserved, not as a luxury but as a necessity: not for 'perfection' so much as for simple 'survival' in the life God has given you."[9] Contemplative rhythms enable us to leave the world in order to not only survive but thrive in it. Let me show you how this has been working out in my own life.

This is the paradox of following Jesus. It's only when we leave the world that we can truly be at home in it.

During a recent personal sabbatical, I decided to fast for nearly four months from all social media (Twitter, Facebook, Instagram). At the beginning of that fast, I set aside four days to be alone with God. As I deleted the apps from my phone, I was already starting to feel anxious. I began to think, *What's going on in the world? What are people saying about me? What bit of information am I missing? Did the Knicks trade for Kevin Durant?* Yes, earth-shattering questions. These thoughts bombarded me for many minutes, revealing my addictive behavior. So in place of the constant flow of information, images, and folly that's found on social media, I decided to cultivate silence in prayer.

I had four days to myself, and at the start of my retreat, I took thirty minutes to close my eyes and be with God. The purpose of this time was not to get anything out of it but simply to be still—to do nothing, say nothing, and just be in God's presence. As I closed my eyes, I began to think about the impact of my ministry, as well as the identity that I have built before others. I saw the ways that I insidiously live according to the value system of the world.

The world says, "Show yourself. Prove your worth. Make a name. Build a platform." I began to think, *Who am I apart from the retweets and likes? Why am I so enamored and preoccupied with the quantity of voices approving and affirming me? How can I say that my identity is grounded in God's love when I give most of my attention to approval of people I've never even met?*

In my time of silent prayer, those questions were answered, but it was in the form of an invitation to leave these questions behind for something altogether different. In this extended period of silence and in my absence from social media, I was disappearing from the world. I was finding myself in another dimension of reality, unaware of what was being spoken of me, whether good or bad, or whether anything was being said about me at all. In a very real sense, I was leaving the world and the grip it had on me. But I was not leaving for good. For a disciple, to leave the world is to enter back into it from another door: the door of God's love and acceptance, the door of God's way of being. This is how, in the leaving, I found myself arriving at home.

Isn't this what you yearn for? Aren't you tired of living at a pace that blurs out beauty, peace, or joy? Don't you want to be at home? The speed we live at does violence against our souls. The inner and outer distractions mini-mize the capacity for us to see God's activity around and within us.

I sometimes imagine a scenario in which someone is locked inside of a supermarket and dies of starvation. Can you imagine? You might say this is impossible. Yet in our spiritual lives, this happens every day. Whether we know it or not, we are locked inside the supermarket of God's abundant life and love. It's all available to us. Even so, people are spiritually starving. But it doesn't have to be this way.

The inner and outer distractions minimize the capacity for us to see God's activity around and within us.

God is committed to our transformation. He is not in the business of simply improving our lives; he wants to infuse them with his life. Every day, he moves toward us in love, reaching, seeking, and pleading with us to pay attention. This is the essence of contemplative rhythms—the goal of monastic life. We have to open ourselves to God's way of being; that is, we have to leave but enter back in through another way. Like the apostle Paul said, we are invited to "live freely, animated and motivated by God's Spirit" (Galatians 5:16, MSG).

But how do we practically flesh this out? In the next chapter, I will explore four indispensable practices that can ground our lives in this slower, more intentional way of contemplative rhythms.

TWO

Deeply Formed Practices of Contemplative Rhythms

Have you ever been scolded by a monk? I have. I recall a convicting conversation I had with Father William Meninger, a well-known Christian monk and one of the founders of the revitalization of silent prayer in monastic settings. He was at our church for a weekend seminar and was to be interviewed on a Sunday morning. Having given himself to a monastic life for decades, Father Meninger has been deeply formed by silent prayer. Much of his daily life is spent in this way.

During the worship gathering, our congregation was passionately singing out the chorus based on Psalm 46:10, "I will be still and know you are God." Immediately following the song, we jumped right into another song and continued with exuberant praise. I was sure the good monk would be impressed with our joyful noise. However, at the end of the service, I was in for a rude awakening.

Father Meninger stood in the church lobby greeting people and taking pictures of all the activity with his massive iPad. He smiled and laughed with everyone he greeted. I looked on all of this with great joy. After twenty minutes of this, I had to escort him back for our second of three Sunday services. That's when his smile and laughter turned into puzzlement.

This monk, an eightysomething-year-old man who had no trouble sharing his thoughts, pulled me aside and asked if he could offer me some feedback on our service. He didn't let me answer, and he didn't wait until we returned to my office. He decided to share his thoughts in the middle of a crowded church lobby. With his eyeglasses sitting at the tip of his nose, and his iPad in hand, he started to lecture me. It was the first time he'd been to our church, and here he was already providing correction.

He said, "You all sang about being still and knowing that God is God. That's great, but why don't you practice what you sing? Why didn't you take a moment to be still?" I was thinking, *Why don't you take a moment to leave, old man?* But I gently smiled and said, "I don't know." He continued to (not so gently) offer words of wisdom about the gift of silence in our worship gatherings. That moment has stuck with me because it reminded me how easy it is to sing about being still but how hard it is to practice it. I was being invited to a deeply formed way of contemplation.

A life formed by contemplative rhythms entails particular practices. Although there are many practices from which to choose, I want to focus on four that have helped me get to know God deeper. I believe they will do the same for you. Furthermore, these practices will prepare you to engage your inner life, racial hostility, your mission, and the ever-present polarization you encounter each day on social media or in your own home. These four contemplative practices are silent prayer, Sabbath keeping, the slow reading of Scripture, and the commitment to stability.

SILENT PRAYER

It's not a stretch to say that our ability to be silent with someone is largely contingent on our level of intimacy or familiarity with that person. My wife, Rosie, and I have been married nearly fifteen years. As we have grown together, so has the ability to enjoy what I'd like to call "bonding silence" with each other. Now, there are those times when we unfortunately can experience that unbonding of the "silent treatment" marked by passive-aggressiveness or anger. I'm not talking about that kind of silence. I'm talking about the quality of silence that we enjoy on long drives, through quiet moments at home, or on a walk together. This is much different from our early dating years.

When Rosie and I first started dating, we had to fill every moment of silence with talking. We were fascinated with each other. We were in a season of discovery, and any kind of silence between us might have been taken as boredom or disinterest and led to some awkwardness. But something changed over the years. While we continue to discover parts about our lives together, we now have (like many couples) the capacity to simply be with each other. The more familiar you are with someone, the easier it is to be silent in that person's presence.

If this general observation is true, this has many implications for our lives with God. One could argue that discomfort with being silent before God just might reveal how unfamiliar we are with God. Christian faith (especially much of the Protestant, Evangelical, and Pentecostal traditions) can be quite noisy. Our Sunday worship gatherings are filled with incessant sound, smothering any opportunity for silence.

Silent prayer is one of the greatest gifts we have to experience a deeply formed life in Christ. At the core of silent prayer is the commitment to establish relationship with God based on friendship rather than demands. Certainly, there is a time to make requests, petition God, and cry out in moments of need. The book of Psalms gives us a clear picture of verbal prayer that is central to life with God. But our verbal prayers best come out of moments of silence that energize and shape our words.

In basic terms, silent prayer is the practice of focusing our attention upon God through the simplicity of shared presence. It's a surrender of our words to be present with the Word (with Jesus).

There's been much talk in our culture about the benefits of mindfulness. The difference between mindfulness and silent prayer is communion with a person. The object of mindfulness is often better psychological and physical health (very important things), but the object of silent prayer is communion with God.

One of my favorite stories about this kind of communion comes from the life of Mother Teresa. During an interview, she was asked what she says to God when she prays. Her answer was, "I don't talk. I simply listen."

Believing he understood what she had just said, the

interviewer next asked, "Ah, then what is it that God says to you when you pray?"

Mother Teresa replied, "He also doesn't talk. He also simply listens."

There was a long silence, with the interviewer seeming a bit confused and not knowing what to ask next. Finally, Mother Teresa broke the silence by saying, "If you can't understand the meaning of what I've just said, I'm sorry, but there's no way I can explain it any better."

I'd like to continue where Mother Teresa left off and offer some words of what this might look like. Contemplative, silent prayer causes us to lay down our preoccupations, for a moment, to tend to the presence and invitation of Jesus, yet this is often a challenging practice. We need a reframing of prayer to get us back on track. Here are four ways forward to cultivate a life of silent prayer.

Focus on Relationship, not Technique

Attitude is key: we must recognize that silent prayer is not a technique to master but a relationship to enter into. I start with this because it's often the case in my life that I want to "do it right." I tend to be a perfectionist by nature, and if I don't master certain things, I tend to just give up. Maybe you identify with my struggle.

Silent prayer is not a technique to master but a relationship to enter into.

In silent prayer, we are constantly called to let go of the need to achieve mastery or to perform well. Whenever I hear of people being recognized spiritual masters, or masters of prayer, I don't think of them as people who have some kind of secret sauce that makes their prayer life extraordinary; I think of them as people who have determined day in and day out to return to the simple act of being with God. There is no such thing as being professionals at prayer. We are always beginners. There are instances when I spend time with God in silence and can sense his love and mercy, but then there are occasions when I feel that it was time wasted. But like with most of our closest relationships, even in the ordinary moments, our shared presence is a gift.

Normalize Boredom

Silent prayer is often uneventful; it's what I refer to as normalized boredom. In a society driven by sensory stimulation, distraction, and activity, silent prayer is an alien practice; it's not from this world. I hope that encourages you. I'm often in conversation with people who lament that nothing earth shattering happens when they are still and silent. I usually say, "Join the club."

Think of boredom during silent prayer as an act of purification. In this uneventful moment, God purifies us of the false god of good feelings. While good feelings are gifts, they can easily become ends in themselves. We can move from worshipping the living God to worshipping our spiritual experiences. This is a fine line we must be mindful of. The ever-urgent need for people growing in relationship with God is the willingness to endure moments that are far from inspirational.

Silent prayer is often something I want to avoid because it forces me to exorcise the demons of excitement, stimulation, and distraction. But it is in these moments that God is truly shaping and forming us. Practicing silent prayer has not been easy, but over time, it has been something I've grown into. There were times of practicing silent prayer for which I could last only a couple of minutes. By God's grace (and a lot of struggle), marking my days with periods of silent prayer (whether for five, ten, or twenty minutes) has deeply formed my life. This kind of prayer, like exercising, often feels impossible in the moment but afterward often provides a great sense of satisfaction.

Reframe Distractions

I used to believe that distraction while in prayer was a sign that I was a bad Christian. As it turns out, distraction in prayer is a sign that I'm a human being. It is impossible to engage in silent prayer without the ongoing wrestling match of the outer and inner voices that besiege us. Distraction, then, becomes a means of reunion with God.

If contemplative, silent prayer ushers us into union with God, distractions inevitably pull us away from this state of being. But they don't have to have the final say. As I heard it said by Thomas Keating, if your mind gets distracted ten thousand times in twenty minutes of prayer, it's "ten thousand opportunities to return to God." Ever since I heard those words, I've seen distraction as an inescapable reality that positions me to come back to God.

We all have to deal with the distracting realities of tasks, responsibilities, and obligations, yet silent prayer is possible even in noisy contexts. Consider, for example, Martha in the famous gospel story in Luke 10:38–42. In this story, Jesus went to the home of Mary, Martha, and Lazarus.

On the surface, the account seems to juxtapose Mary the contemplative with Martha the activist. Martha was actively trying to feed everyone and, in the process, became indignantly resentful at her sister, who was just sitting at Jesus's feet. In her annoyance, she even began to boss Jesus around, saying, "Tell her then to help me" (verse 40). In that moment, Jesus tenderly acknowledged how worried, distracted, and upset Martha was. But he let her know that Mary had chosen what was better at that moment and that only one thing was necessary: attentive presence.

When we read this passage, the usual interpretation is that we are to be prayerful like Mary and resist working frenetically like Martha. But perhaps there's another way of viewing this. Like Martha, Jesus had plenty of moments of nonstop activity, yet he remained anchored in attentive presence with his Father. Perhaps the issue with Martha is not her busyness but her lack of inner attentiveness. As West African theologian Robert Sarah wrote,

> Jesus rebukes Martha, not for being busy in the kitchen—after all she did have to prepare the meal—but for her inattentive interior attitude, betrayed by her annoyance with her sister. . . . Christ tenderly invites her to stop so as to return to her heart, the place of true welcome and the dwelling place of God's silent tenderness, from which she had been led away by the activity to which she was devoting herself so noisily.[1]

Our distractions, whether in the moment of silent prayer or in the moment of steady demands, do not need to ruin our lives with God. Our distractions become invitations to return, ever so silently, back to the center of God's heart.

Remember That God Is Always Waiting with Open Arms

Along these lines, engaging in silent prayer requires us to remember that God is always for us. One of the reasons we don't come to prayer is because we believe that God is angry with us. We dare not approach the throne of grace with boldness because we have been ravaged by guilt and shame. And even if we come to God, we don't believe we deserve to be there.

Minister Marjorie Thompson captured this well: "Our twisted inner logic, often unconscious, can convince us that we are too bad even for God to forgive! To hold God's mercy hostage to a determination to punish ourselves is truly a human sickness of spirit."[2]

The beauty of Christian spirituality is that the God we are in relationship with is for us in Christ. Like the father in the prodigal son story, God is waiting with his eyes looking for us in the distance. He is waiting to embrace us. This image might take some getting used to, but it's one we need to remind ourselves of constantly. God just wants us home.

When we closely examine the story of the prodigal son, we see an image of love that is to shape our image of God. The prodigal son doesn't return with a renewed love for his father; he comes back simply to survive. And his father is perfectly fine with that. God just wants us home.

SABBATH KEEPING

Sabbath keeping is a weekly twenty-four-hour period of unhurried delight with no have-tos or ought-tos, resulting in deep rest and renewal. The contemplative life is about slowing down our pace to create space for God to transform us by his grace. So it only makes sense that keeping the Sabbath is another indispensable practice.

The fact is, humanity needs to keep the Sabbath, as many in our world are regularly on the brink of burnout. For example, the Japanese government is deciding whether to make it mandatory for workers to take five days of vacation per year:

> Japan has long had a reputation for being one of the most overworked countries in the world. The term *karoshi*, or death by overwork, emerged in the 1990s when an increasing number of Japanese professionals were dying from heart attacks and strokes. Recent years have seen an epidemic of suicide, in part because of work-related stress: of 30,000 suicides in 2011, 10,000 were believed to be related to over-work.[3]

This extreme and sad report should cause us to take a hard look at our lives. Although we might take vacation time in a given year, we still tend to be a tired, exhausted people. The fatigue we experience is multilayered.

There is the *fatigue of the body*. We don't get as much sleep as we need. We push our bodies to the limit and live off cups of coffee and Red Bull. There is also the *fatigue of the mind.* In a given day, we are bombarded with cease-less information that we have no time to absorb or pro-cess. And ultimately, there is the *fatigue of the soul.* We are people who have little margin to be with God and foster a life-giving rhythm for the long haul.

Sabbath is an invitation to a life that isn't dominated and distorted by overwork.

That is why we need Sabbath. It's why God modeled it in his creation. Sabbath is an invitation to a life that isn't dominated and distorted by overwork. This feeling of domination and distortion is something we know all too well, and by "all," I mean all of humanity. You could argue that the commandment most violated by everyone is the fourth. It's also the commandment we often boast about breaking in our pride to express how tirelessly we work. Yet our lives are under the judgment of our own frenetic pace because we can't stop.

Our story echoes that of the people of Israel. The command of Sabbath keeping was first stated in the Ten Commandments (see Exodus 20), and there are two im-portant things to know right off the top. First, the Ten Commandments were given not as a *means* of salvation but as the result of salvation. In other words, God never intended them to be the means by which people enter into relationship with him. He first rescued his people out of Egypt and *then* gave them the commandments. He didn't give them commandments to live out perfectly as a condition leading to their rescue, like for most other religions, which are often based on human performance.

The story of Scripture is not really about human performance so much as it is about how God has performed over and over for his people. This is good news for all of us. God's care and love for you is not based on how well you perform and live. His love always comes first and is unconditional. The reason the Ten Commandments are given is because they would become a way of life that describes what redeemed people look and live like.

Note the attention given to each commandment; you'll see immediately that the fourth has a good deal of commentary. Why does the fourth take up so much more space in the Bible? Here's what might be happening.

For four hundred years, the people of God had one identity: they were slaves. And it was the job of slaves to work. Their very existence was predicated on their ability to work. The famous philosopher René Descartes coined the phrase "I think, therefore I am," but for the people of Israel, their lives were instead defined by this: "I work, therefore I am." Their fundamental identity was related to work. And because work was nonstop, they had no clue how to live any other way. You might have experienced the same thing in your life.

From a very early age, one of the first questions children are asked is, "What do you want to be when you grow up?" When that question is presented, we are not necessarily thinking about character or virtues; we are thinking about career, vocation, or work. It's not a bad question, but let's just call it what it is: we tend to be overly preoccupied with work.

Biblically, work is inherently a good thing. God worked at creation and made humans to do the same. Work was established before sin entered the world. But one of the major problems we all face is overwork. In our fallen state, work very easily becomes a powerful force that crowds out any kind of connection with God (which is arguably at the heart of the original sin: independence from God).

Our obsession with work has predictably made us destructive people. For many in our society, overwork is about not just obsession but also oppression—that is, the various factors that force a person to work so much. Tragically, many people have no choice but to work endlessly, often at multiple jobs. My point is, whether by obsession or oppression, we live a destructive way of life. The kind of destruction I'm talking about is against our bodies and souls and, consequently, against others.

Our struggle with overwork is an ancient one, and the remedy requires an ancient wisdom. In the midst of the exhausting, busy, and frantic lives we live, God gives us the gift of the Sabbath. And the brilliance of Sabbath keeping is that it's not so much about our keeping the Sabbath as it is the Sabbath keeping us.

The Sabbath reminds us of the gospel of grace. In actuality, Sabbath keeping might be the greatest sign of grace because it's while we are intentionally accomplishing nothing that God loves us. This, indeed, is good news. To follow are four reminders about Sabbath keeping.

Sabbath Is Not a Reward Earned for Hard Work

We live in a legalistic world that says, "If you want to rest, you better work." In other words, work first, then rest. Because this is the order of our culture, we often believe that Sabbath is a reward for hard work. People who think along these lines believe that the only way to deserve a Sabbath is by working until they have no energy left. They often think of grace in the same terms, as if God's favor is something one should strive to be deserving of; that is, "You've been given it, now earn it." God's point is, earning is altogether irrelevant to love. Likewise, you don't earn (let alone deserve) the favor in Sabbath.

When I first tried learning about Sabbath, I often felt guilty taking one if I wasn't exhausted. Some of us come from families who feel that way. Some of us come from families who immigrated to this country and had to work nonstop to survive. We grew up in these homes and the message was clear: rest is a reward. Oftentimes the reason this is emphasized is that we are mindful of laziness. But I want you to know that Sabbath is not a reward for hard work. Sabbath is a gift that precedes work and enables us to work.

Just look at the first day of rest. God created the world in six days (see Genesis 1). On the sixth day, he created Adam and Eve. Their first day was the seventh day, which was the day God created rest. They began with a Sabbath, out of which they worked.

As with God's grace, rest is never a reward; it's a gift.

Sabbath Is a Reminder That Our Work Remains Incomplete

One of the more painful realities of Sabbath keeping is that some of our work will remain incomplete. We often tell ourselves, *When I finish everything, then I will rest.* But when does it end? There's always more work to be done. Consequently, the pressure and anxiety we feel about the incomplete work is one of the biggest obstacles to keeping Sabbath. I know this firsthand.

Often on Friday evenings as our family Sabbath is about to begin, I'll remember something I forgot to do—maybe an email I forgot to send or a phone call I forgot to make—and I'll be tempted to keep working until I get the task done, even though I know there's always another thing to do. One of my favorite metaphors in this regard for Sabbath keeping is from the Food Network.

On the network's cooking-competition shows, all chefs have a certain amount of time to prepare their meals. As the time comes to an end, no matter where they are in the process, once the buzzer sounds, the chefs have to put their hands in the air. They can't add a twig of parsley, reposition the caramelized brussels sprouts, sprinkle a little powdered sugar—nothing. They must step away from the plate. In the same way, when Sabbath begins, we'd do well to raise our hands and step away from our devices, the office, or wherever and by whatever means we are working.

In the practice of Sabbath keeping, we live out the truth that one day we will leave all things unfinished as we rest in the arms of Jesus.

Sabbath Is a Day That Moves Us from Production to Presence

A young doctor finishes her psychiatry residency and begins working in a New York City hospital. A friend of hers, also a doctor, who is a few years ahead of her and pregnant with her second child, asks, "Do you know what I love most about being pregnant?" She then shares, "I love being pregnant because it's the only time I feel productive all the time. Even if I'm sleeping, I'm doing something."

Sabbath is not just rest from making things. It's rest from the need to make something of ourselves.

We are often so used to producing that we forget to be present. The Sabbath, then, is a day of presence—a day of being present to God, present to others, present to creation, and present to ourselves. It is certainly true that keeping Sabbath might make us more productive. But we keep Sabbath not because it makes us more productive at work but to resist the idol of productivity. We are more than what we produce.

Sabbath is not just rest from making things. It's rest from the need to make something of ourselves. It's a day of noticing, a day of simple joyful presence, which is why community and eating together are such good Sabbath practices. It's a day of presence.

Sabbath creates a space for a holy unawareness in a world of technological omniscience. Sabbath forms us to be present in one place amid the desire to be omnipresent. Sabbath shapes us to enjoy the limits of our humanity rather than grasp at omnipotence.

Sabbath Points Us to the Deeper Rest We Need

Sabbath keeping is not just about a practice; it's about a person. More than anything else, the Sabbath reminds us about the true rest we need: soul rest. We live our entire lives trying to make a name for ourselves, trying to become something, working hard to be noticed, or proving that we matter. And all of this is exhausting, isn't it?

There is a quality of rest that our souls need that goes beyond a spiritual-formation practice. There's a quality of rest we need that is more than ceasing from work. The quality of rest we need is from God alone. Jesus affirmed it this way: "Come to me, all you who are weary and burdened, and I will give you rest" (Matthew 11:28, NIV). The way to experiencing this kind of rest is not found in something we do; it's found in something God has done. Jesus Christ underwent the biggest kind of rest imaginable: he rested in a tomb after being crucified. But as he rested, the world was being renewed; as he rested, the world was being restored; and as he rested, the world was about to see resurrection. And here's the promise: when we place our faith in Jesus, we exchange our exhaustion for his rest.

I'd like to pull this all together with a New York City example of how my family (my wife and two kids) and I practice Sabbath keeping. We start our Sabbath every Friday at 6:00 p.m. and observe it until Saturday at 6:00 p.m. (if I weren't a pastor, I would observe it Saturday through Sunday to include worship at church). We kick it off by lighting a candle on our dining room table. The candle simply reminds us of God's presence and the gift of rest.

In our home, Sabbath means we stop all our paid work. We stop our unpaid work as well (laundry, grocery shopping, and other household chores, though we do feed our family. Have you tried fasting with a six-year-old boy?). Unpaid work might differ from person to person, but the point is, if it constitutes work, we should do all we can to let it go. Our Sabbath over the twenty-four-hour period is marked by us resting, playing, and intentionally doing the things that bring us joy. For us this means dinner with friends and family, playing basketball, reading, napping, and taking in some of the sights of our city.

It's important for me to say that with two young kids, Sabbath is not always stress free. I don't know about the kids in your life, but mine don't automatically turn into angels just because the Sabbath has come. On some Saturday nights, I feel as tired as when I started the Sabbath because of the responsibilities of parenting, but more often than not I feel refreshed. That said, I'm confident that with some reflection and conversation with those closest to you, you can start the Sabbath-keeping journey. Like with all the practices, give yourself a lot of grace and space to experiment.

SLOW READING OF SCRIPTURE

The third deeply formed practice for building contemplative rhythm is the slow reading of Scripture. It's undeniable that we find ourselves in a skimming, speed-reading, scrolling culture. This consumption culture has profoundly influenced the way we engage (or don't engage) holy Scripture. Instead of slowly ingesting the truth of God's written Word, we live on the surface of the text, rarely settled enough to hear God's particular word to us in the particular season of our lives. This is why Psalm 1 serves as a much-needed corrective word to us.

If you've read any of the psalms, you'll notice how different the first psalm is from the other 149. Psalm 1 is not a prayer, but it's a statement about human existence. It is basically the gateway to true prayer and communion with God. The psalmist begins by making a staggering statement: the primary thing that distinguishes the righteous from the unrighteous is meditation on the law. When I speak of the slow reading of Scripture, I have in mind this practice of meditation the psalmist introduces. The righteous are those who are directed by God's instruction. The unrighteous in this psalm have no room for his instruction in their lives.

The topic of meditation might seem distant to people unfamiliar with spiritual practices, but whether you know it or not, you have meditated before. Let me give you an example. If you've ever received a love letter or note from someone, surely you have meditated. I remember getting a text message from Rosie after one of our first dates in 2003. It made me feel really special. The text couldn't have been longer than two sentences, but I read it again and again. I showed my coworkers what she said. I opened my Nokia flip phone repeatedly to read it. I was meditating on her words.

Maybe you've received a very encouraging and affirming email from someone you highly regard. The words called forth feelings of joy and appreciation. Chances are that you spent time replaying those words in your head. Or perhaps you received a harsh, critical word that hurt you. We all know what it's like to chew on someone's negative words over and over again. What we are doing in those moments is meditating.

My favorite example of meditation, however, comes from dogs. Dogs have a lot to teach us about meditating. Eugene Peterson, in his book *Eat This Book,* tells the story of his dog chewing, playing, and growling over a bone that would sometimes last it more than a week. One day Peterson read Isaiah 31:4, which says that the Lord is like a young lion growling over its prey. He immediately thought of his growling, joyful dog playing with its bone. He then discovered a connection: the Hebrew word for "growl" was the same word for "meditate" in Psalm 1.[4] This becomes a powerful metaphor for shaping the way we approach Scripture. Meditation, then, is the practice of slowly chewing on God's Word until it penetrates our hearts.

The question now is, how do we do it? It's here where I turn to a practice many in the church have cultivated for centuries. It's called *lectio divina*. It simply means sacred reading, and it's a practice of slowing down and chewing on Scripture through four movements: *lectio, meditatio, oratio,* and *contemplatio;* that is, reading, meditation, prayer, and contemplation.

Lectio: Reading

The first movement is *lectio,* which means reading. But this is not a careless, flippant, perfunctory kind of reading. It's attentive reading. It's reading for the purpose of an encounter with God. In the first movement of lectio, there is a recognition that Scripture "is alive and active. Sharper than any double-edged sword, it penetrates even to dividing soul and spirit, joints and marrow" (Hebrews 4:12, NIV).

In lectio, we approach holy Scripture not as an object but as a subject. It's more than ancient words on a page. Scripture is not to be approached as an object of our inquiry but as an animating force setting its gaze on us. As we read Scripture, we come to understand that God is reading *us*. In this first movement, then, we ask the Lord to help us locate a word or phrase in a short passage of Scripture as we read it two or three times. As we read, we ask, "Lord, what does it say?"

Meditatio: Meditation

The second movement is *meditatio,* which means meditation. In this movement, we are particularly focused on the word or phrase that one believes has been identified by the Spirit for this moment. Like it was for the dog Eugene Peterson wrote of, this is the time to "growl" over the text. We chew on the word or phrase, reflecting on what God might want to say to us. Perhaps there's a situation or relationship that needs addressing. The word or phrase energized by the Spirit begins to form our hearts and wills. In this moment, we are essentially asking, "Lord, what are you saying to me?"

Oratio: Prayer

The third movement is *oratio,* which means prayer. In meditation, we are aware of God's Word being spoken to our hearts. In *oratio,* we reciprocate that movement, now offering words to God from our hearts. In *oratio,* we speak freely to God (whether verbally or in writing), calling out the ways we have been addressed. In this movement, the emphasis is on our responses to God's gracious initiative. In this moment, we ask ourselves, "What do I want to say to God?"

Contemplatio: Contemplation

The final movement is *contemplatio,* which means contemplation. Much like the practice of silent prayer, contemplation in this moment is not for the purpose of further rumination and examination. God has spoken to us. We have spoken in return. Now we are called to simply rest in God's abiding love. No more questions are required.

Unless we are immersing ourselves in Scripture for the purpose of being encountered by God (not merely observing the text), we will find our formations in Christ limited. God has spoken in Jesus and has spoken through his written Word. We are invited to slowly enter into that world.

COMMITMENT TO STABILITY

Contemplative life is not a solo enterprise; it is an invitation to a shared life with others. This is one of the great lessons we can learn from monastic communities. Monks who enter a monastery take a vow of stability that grounds them in certain places for life. On some level, this vow is a manifestation of their commitment to silent prayer. In silent prayer, we are called to withstand the inner disturbances and annoyances of ourselves for the sake of union with God. In a commitment to stability, we withstand the disturbances and annoyances of others for the sake of union with God and union with each other.

Yet this is no easy task. In a church culture dominated by a church-shopping transience, choosing to remain for the long haul is a modern-day miracle. (Sadly, many people remain in settings given to spiritual abuse, theological toxicity, and interpersonal dysfunction. When this is the environment, one would do well to find a healthy community.) I'm referring to our call to remain connected with others, especially in moments of conflict, tension, and anxiety. The goal of contemplation is beholding, but not only a beholding of God; we also need to be beholding each other.

THREE

Racial Reconciliation for a Divided World

"The real question of Christian discipleship is not can I be your brother in Christ, but can I be your brother-in-law?" I first heard this statement in a seminary class. Who can't your child marry? Who do you feel uneasy about having in your home? Questions like these help us get to the core of our racial situations. It's one thing to be in close proximity to someone who looks, thinks, or even eats differently than you; it's another to be in deep relationship with that person, and still another to work for a world (that is, Christ's kingdom) in which our differences are not placed on a hierarchy that regards some as superior and others as inferior.

Racial sin and hostility in our world is very real. In the United States, places and names such as Ferguson, Eric Garner, Trayvon Martin, George Floyd, and Charlottesville have reminded us that matters of race remain one of America's deeply embedded thorns in the flesh. Just take a look at your social media timeline. A day doesn't go by when we don't see people vocalizing their rage, puzzlement, and defensiveness over matters of race. The turbulent discourse has found its way into our local churches and our homes.

We are consistently faced with the troubles of a racialized world. The stories we hear and see seem to be endless. Whether the stories are nationally televised or known only to us, we are regularly weighed down by the destructive ideas and practices that establish subtle and not-so-subtle hierarchies of human value based on skin color. Although the symbols of racism have been largely dismantled, the spirit of racism continues to permeate our world.

But we are not without help. There is a way that can take us beyond the disjointed and narrow approaches that fail to engage the multiple perspectives of racism—perspectives that include our collective past, our inner lives, and our outward engagement. This chapter and the next will provide a succinct, multilayered look and strategy to help us respond to one of the biggest challenges to deeply formed spiritual living.

TENSIONS IN BROOKLYN

During my childhood, the East New York section of Brooklyn was one of the most dangerous and economically poor areas of New York City. I grew up around Puerto Ricans, Dominicans, Jamaicans, and African Americans. Certainly, there were tensions between these groups, but one consistent place of racial and ethnic conflict was

Chinese take-out restaurants or the local Korean-owned dry cleaners. I can vividly recall the tension as well as the glimmers of healing that would surface from time to time. I have one memory in particular.

As a teenager and into my twenties, I would make monthly trips to the dry cleaners. For as long as I can remember, there was a massive bulletproof partition on the counter that separated the customer from the dry-cleaner employee. In order to drop the clothes off, one had to put the clothes into a drop box and then talk through the clear partition, giving specific instructions. I thought all this was normal until the day the partition was removed. One day in my midtwenties, I stopped in to drop off a few button-down shirts, and to my great surprise the partition had been taken down. I was about to go back outside to make sure I was in the same place. I mentioned how different the store looked and the owner said, in his heavy accent, "We want to build trust with our neighbors." For the first time, I was able to shake hands with someone in that space.

Upon reflection of that situation, I couldn't help but think that something deeply spiritual had taken place on the corner in that neighborhood. I would find out later that the new Korean owners of that business were Christians. Something had compelled them to imagine a different way of being together. A new community was forming based not on suspicion, mistrust, and fear but on hospitality, trust, and goodwill. In that small dry-cleaner's space, a metaphor of the gospel became clear as day. It wasn't the fall of the Berlin Wall, but in my neighborhood, it was a significant act.

> The Cross of Christ isn't just a bridge that
> gets us to God; it's a sledgehammer that
> breaks down walls that separate us.

You see, God is not simply in the business of dry cleaning our souls; he is in the business of tearing down walls and creating a new family, a new way of belonging together. One could argue that the primary fruit of the gospel is not going to heaven when you die but rather the miraculous new family that is created out of the death and resurrection of Jesus. Racial justice and reconciliation remain two of the most urgent matters of faith and public witness. In this respect, the Cross of Christ isn't just a bridge that gets us to God; it's a sledgehammer that breaks down walls that separate us.

In the midst of all the confusion and anger that persist due to the racial tensions in our country and world, the church must lead the way in proclaiming a message of hope, justice, and reconciliation. This is what we have attempted to do at New Life Fellowship.

THE STORY OF NEW LIFE

New Life Fellowship Church was planted in 1987 by an Italian American New Yorker named Pete Scazzero. After a radical conversion to Christ, Pastor Pete (as our congregation affectionately calls him) was exposed to a variety of church traditions and theologies. Soon after, he gained a vision of the gospel's power to tear down walls and work for reconciliation. Pete became a staff worker with InterVarsity Christian Fellowship at Rutgers University and immersed himself in a campus community committed to seeing Jesus reconcile all things. After his time with InterVarsity was over, Pete went on to study Spanish in Costa Rica. He felt a deep call to plant a local church in Queens, and he wanted to reach as many people in the neighborhood as he could.

To practice his Spanish, Pete served in small Latino congregations in Queens until he felt ready to plant New Life. New Life grew rapidly, and within a few years, there was an English-speaking congregation as well as a Spanish-speaking one. Pete led them both. The full story of this, as well as the subsequent crisis (and transformation), is detailed in his two books *The Emotionally Healthy Church* and *Emotionally Healthy Spirituality*.[1]

Studies show that half of Queens is foreign born. At one point, the area where our church building is located was deemed the most diverse zip code in the world by National Geographic. As I mentioned earlier, there are at least seventy-five nationalities represented in our church. People from more than one hundred countries have been through the health center that's operated through our New Life Community Development Corporation. Well over a hundred languages are spoken in the local hospital. To withdraw twenty dollars from the local ATM is a dizzying effort, as there are often fifteen languages to choose from. In short, New Life (and our neighborhood) is a beautiful community to be in, yet it requires a lot of cultural flexibility to navigate well.

The gift to our local church community is that we get an opportunity to experience the beauty and richness of cultures from around the world. The challenge of our local church is that we must come to terms with the global and national tensions that exist and how these tensions find their way into our community. If there's conflict on the world stage, we feel it at New Life. Wherever tragedy strikes, for example, the Philippines, Indonesia, Venezuela, or Greece, many of our congregants are personally affected. When the World Cup or Olympics comes around, watch out. When South Korea beat Germany in the World Cup in 2018, I don't think the Koreans and Germans were praying with each other for a while. To add to this complexity, we regularly come across differing views related to the current state of political life. Every week is an opportunity to be swept up in the collective antagonisms of a deeply polarized world.

In our church, we have #blacklivesmatter activists and #alllivesmatter advocates. Pro-Trump and never-Trump voters sit next to each other every Sunday (often unbeknownst to each other). We have people who see everything through the lens of a racialized society, and we have immigrants who don't fully grasp what all the fuss is about. We have people who want every other sermon to be on dismantling racism, and we have folks who are triggered anytime race is brought up. I've received emails from people leaving our church because the sermons came across as too focused on race and not the gospel, and I've been chastised by people desiring greater focus on the current events that are dominating the racial conversation. There are moments when I step back and see the hand of Jesus forming our community. There are other moments when it seems as though evil powers are wreaking havoc among our church family.

Over the years, we have learned to grow together and draw out powerful truths about the nature of the gospel in the context of racial justice and reconciliation. No one can truly understand New Life apart from this commitment that informs all we do. I'd like to offer some ways we have sought to shape our diverse community through theological clarity and spiritual formation depth.[2]

CREATION OF A NEW FAMILY

The starting point for any Christian conversation on race must be the purpose of the gospel. The gospel we proclaim must be big enough to engage the realities of racial fragmentation. However, it's often not seen this way. Sadly, there is often a hyperspiritual perspective held by many Christians who see racial justice and reconciliation as optional or ancillary to the gospel.

> The gospel we proclaim must be big enough to engage the realities of racial fragmentation.

For many, the gospel is their ticket to the afterlife: "When I die, I go to heaven because of what Jesus has done for me." For others, the gospel is connected to a particular understanding of the death and resurrection of Jesus. Along this line of thinking, the gospel is reduced to a particular theology of atonement. Herein lies one of our greatest challenges.

When the essence of the gospel is stripped down to

the afterlife or to a glorious but strictly individual personal decision of faith, it's not what Jesus described as the good news about his kingdom come. And predictably, there's no real urgency to see lives oriented toward a more loving and just way of being in the world. Our understanding of the gospel will be either Christ's kingdom catalyst for racial justice and reconciliation, or a conformity to this world's impetus for a fragmented and divided society. Surely, the gospel is good news, but good news about what?

It is my conviction that the gospel at its core is not merely the good news of a soteriological transaction (a fancy way of saying "getting saved"). The gospel at its core is centrally about the story and victory of Jesus; the risen and enthroned Lord is our good news. And further, this gospel has specific purposes for the healing of our world. One of the main purposes is the creation of a new family that transcends racial and ethnic barriers.

Along these lines, North American theologian George Eldon Ladd, in his short but seminal book on the gospel of the kingdom, wrote, "The Gospel must not only offer a personal salvation in the future life to those who believe; it must also transform all of the relationships of life here and now and thus cause the Kingdom of God to prevail in all the world."[3]

At the core of the gospel, then, is the "making right" of all things through Jesus. In Jesus's death and resurrection, the world is set on a trajectory of renewal, but God graciously invites us to work toward this future. However, this work is not an individual enterprise; it is one orchestrated by the collected efforts of a new family in the power of the Spirit. What this means is that God is not simply in the business of saving souls; he is in the business of creating a new family. We see this new family early on in the Gospels in Jesus's calling of his disciples. In the building of this new family of twelve, we see the power of the gospel at work.

The gathering of the twelve disciples is a far cry from what most of us experience, especially on social media. Although the symbols are long gone (segregated water fountains, schools, and restaurants), we live in a world that is becoming more segmented and more segregated.

> God is not simply in the business of saving souls; he is in the business of creating a new family.

In a *Fast Company* article, the term *filter bubble* describes an algorithm on Facebook that created an echo chamber for people to see only the content they would most likely agree with.[4] The filter bubble is a good image for what is happening in our time. We surround ourselves with ideas, interests, and political thoughts that reinforce what we already believe. This has led to a brazen demonizing of people who think otherwise.

The way of this current world is to friend and follow people in the social media universe based on shared interests and values. Although this brings about helpful social identification and connection based on affinity, it has created a new set of problems. We are increasingly distanced from people with whom we disagree. But this was not Jesus's approach.

In the calling of his disciples, Jesus put people together who would most certainly not follow each other
on Twitter. Yet in the forming of this small community,
he was symbolically making a statement that in the kingdom of God, a new family was being created. A quick
glance at two of the disciples brings out this truth. Consider Matthew and Simon the Zealot (see Matthew 10:3–
4). Matthew worked for the government; Simon hated
the government. Matthew was a tax collector; Simon was
a tax *protester.* Matthew collected revenue for the Romans; Simon was a rebel against the Romans. Matthew
was wealthy; Simon was working class. Matthew made a
living taking advantage of people like Simon; Simon
made a living trying to kill people like Matthew.

Despite all these differences, somehow Matthew and
Simon were able to remain connected. But it cost them
something. Matthew had to stop taking advantage of
people like Simon; Simon had to embrace a different vision of revolution. This is the essence of the new family
Jesus was creating. Reconciliation in community will always cost us something, and in Christ the barriers that
separate us can come down in his name.

Beyond the original twelve, Jesus would invite women
to be his disciples. He would give the disciples the charge
to reach non-Jewish people. In the book of Acts, the
Holy Spirit led the church to see this vision realized as a
new family was forged—not based on ethnic or gender
identity but through the death and resurrection of Jesus.
In the New Testament, familial language is used throughout. Men and women are seen as brothers and sisters.
Those who belong to Jesus have God not as distant creator but as Abba ("father"). We are all given a new family

inheritance. This is language of the new creation of a family, transcending ethnic, cultural, and generational differences. It's a family marked by reconciliation.

RECONCILIATION

Reconciliation is an important word. It's a biblical word. However, in recent years, I've had some ambivalence about using it, due to the ways it has been stripped of its power in certain contexts. It's often watered down to mean "surface diversity." But reconciliation is more than that.

I have found pastor and author Dr. Brenda Salter McNeil's definition incredibly helpful. She succinctly captured the multifaceted nature of biblical reconciliation: "Reconciliation is an ongoing spiritual process involving forgiveness, repentance and justice that restores broken relationships and systems to reflect God's original intention for all creation to flourish."[5] In this definition, Dr. McNeil underscored a number of realities that must be engaged for true reconciliation to take place; namely, the personal and public dimensions of it.

The Gospel at Work Amid Racial Hostility

In order to work for peace and wholeness amid racial hostility, it's important to get a handle on terms. I'm convinced that so much of the misunderstandings related to this conversation are related to our inability to get clear on language. Before offering a way forward in our individual and community lives, a bit of nuance here is important. I have found speaker and activist Lisa Sharon Harper's simple delineation of terms helpful, as she dis-

tinguished race, ethnicity, culture, and nationality from a
biblical perspective:

> *Race, ethnicity, culture,* and *nationality* often
> are used as interchangeable words, but each
> one has a different shade of meaning. . . .
>
> *Ethnicity* is biblical (Hebrew: *goy* or *am;*
> Greek: *ethnos*). Ethnicity is created by God as
> people groups move together through space
> and time. . . .
>
> *Culture* is implicit in Scripture, but the word
> itself is never used. Culture is a sociological and
> anthropological term that refers to the beliefs,
> norms, rituals, arts, and worldviews of particu-
> lar people groups in a particular place at a par-
> ticular time. Culture is fluid. . . .
>
> *Nationality* indicates the sovereign nation/
> state where an individual is a legal citizen. It is
> a geopolitical category determined by the legal
> structures of the state. . . .
>
> Race is about power—in political terms, *do-*
> *minion.* As a political construct, race was created
> by humans to determine who can exercise power
> within a governing structure and to guide deci-
> sions regarding how to allocate resources.[6]

My focus in this chapter is on the racial and ethnic
categories, and in order to engage it thoroughly and with
integrity, we must see this conversation happening in
spaces both individual and institutional. To examine race
matters in this way requires us to take a hard look at ourselves and the ways we've been formed. American novel-

ist James Baldwin observed, "Not everything that is faced can be changed, but nothing can be changed until it is faced."[7] As we examine the multilayered reality of race, we will be better equipped to offer theologically grounded responses to see the new family of Jesus flourish all over the world.

Individual Racial Prejudice

When I was in high school in Queens, there were regular tensions between Puerto Ricans and Dominicans. If you wanted to offend a Puerto Rican, you could just call that person a Dominican and vice versa. I remember walking down the crowded school hallways with Puerto Rican friends, and predictably someone pointed at an unassuming kid from the Dominican Republic and stereotypically insulted him about his clothes, his noticeable accent, or whether he was documented or not.

As I look back on those days, we all could have passed for cousins. But racial prejudice runs deep. At the core of racism is the lie that some people are superior or inferior to others. This happens across all different people groups. Each of us has our prejudices, and the vast majority (if not all of us) have been formed by an "ism" of this world that creates barriers between us and others (classism, racism, ethnocentrism, sexism, ageism).

We are all shaped by a particular history and context and formed by family, friends, and the media. This means we carry blind spots and biases. To discriminate is not necessarily a bad thing (it's wise to be discriminating in whom you trust as a close friend, for instance). However, discrimination that makes some humans out to be superior or inferior to others is a dangerous lie and destructive sin.

To do the work of racial reconciliation is to take ownership of the marginalizing ways we see others who are in some form or another different from us. One of the biggest challenges in the conversation on race is our refusal to do the work of identifying and exposing our individual racial prejudice. We have been socialized to see people in certain ways. This is a problem for all of us regardless of our skin color.

However, historically not all racial bias has the same social impact. The racial bias in the hands of people of color is quite different from racial bias in the hands of the dominant culture. In the dominant culture, racial prejudice morphs into racism in larger institutional and societal ways. Individual racial prejudice is about how we negatively and often violently *perceive* others, but institutional racism is about how *power* is used.

Institutional Racism

In my work as a pastor, I've noticed how conversations about institutional racism are much more difficult to navigate. In America, many like to believe that if individuals work hard enough, they can transcend limitations and reach their dreams. In truth, though, our value of individualism blinds us to the injustices from which some benefit at the expense of others. I'm aware of this in my congregational context. After I had preached a sermon on institutional racism, one of our congregants—a kind, generous older White man—approached me in the lobby and whispered, "Rich, please don't lump me in with those people. I never owned a slave." What this dear brother failed to see was that although he never owned a slave, he benefits from a history that has positioned White men to be on the top of our racialized world.

Institutional racism grants advantages to some and disadvantages to others, often in ways we cannot see. We are accustomed to thinking about racism in its most blatant culturally unacceptable manifestations. We think about the Ku Klux Klan, racial slurs, burning crosses, and the like. But institutional racism is often hidden in plain sight.

The strategy for working for reconciliation requires a gospel big enough to address our individual racial prejudice (which affects everyone) as well as the systemic misuse of power (which affects those with low social power). To get at some of the institutional racism in our world, this diagram may be of some help:

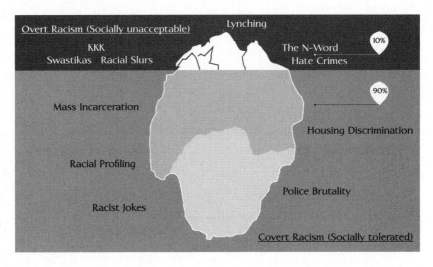

What this diagram communicates is the truth that institutional racism is a multifaceted problem often not seen with our eyes. Paul wrote about invisible powers and principalities that are at work in our world (see Ephe-

sians 6:12). Scripture identifies a triumvirate axis of evil
that is all spiritual: flesh-and-blood human individuals,
incorporeal beings (demons), and the evils embodied in
the structures and collective consciousness of what Scripture calls "this present darkness."

Just as with spiritual beings, not everyone believes or
acknowledges that the world system exists. Some see institutional racism as obvious, while others refuse to give
it any credence. Not surprisingly, the divide reflects the
racial assumptions about the nature of morality, responsi-
bility, and sin. In one of his incisive articles, sociologist
Dr. Michael Emerson remarked, "Whites tend to view
racism as intended individual acts of overt prejudice and
discrimination. . . . Most people of color define racism
quite differently. [For people of color], racism is, at a
minimum, prejudice plus power, and that power comes
not from being a prejudiced individual, but from being
part of a group that controls the nation's systems."[8]

In truth, both individual racism and systemic racism
are our realities. But systemic/institutional racism is a way
that power in a society is ordered to give advantage to
some and disadvantage to others. In the United States,
institutional racism emerges from a sinful hierarchy that
normalizes and prioritizes White people, and this might be
hard to receive. But the residue of White normativity and
White supremacy remains deeply at work in our society.

This way of understanding life is often protested by
people who have believed in the narrative of the American Dream. The notion of institutional racism is also
hotly contested by people who might be part of the dominant culture from a racial or economic perspective. So
when I say we need to wrestle with race from an institu-

tional perspective, my thinking is first of all informed by the biblical story of sin and then shaped by historical and sociological data. The prophetic books in the Old Testament take on both the systemic and structural natures of sin. Let's look at one passage in particular.

Systemic, Institutional Sin in the Bible

One of the many reasons we need to read the Prophets is because they speak to the public dimension of God's love. Many of us have experienced the personal or private dimension of God's love; we know what it's like to receive his grace and kindness personally. But the prophets remind us that God's love is not just a private affair. As American philosopher Dr. Cornel West said, "Justice is what love looks like in public."[9]

In Isaiah 10, we see words about a miscarriage of justice in the public life of the people of God, and Isaiah couldn't remain silent. In the first two verses, he wrote, "Woe to those who decree iniquitous decrees, and the writers who keep writing oppression, to turn aside the needy from justice and to rob the poor of my people of their right, that widows may be their spoil, and that they may make the fatherless their prey!"

The cry of Isaiah is for righteousness—for justice. And justice very simply is about having right relationships, one with another. To do justice means that every person is taken seriously as a human being made in the image of God. So Isaiah wrote these prophetic words because the people who were in charge of ensuring that society was ordered toward justice were doing the opposite. Isaiah cried out against the larger structures of human existence. Isaiah was basically saying that on an institutional level, people were being sinned against. There were unjust laws that were oppressing people. Justice was being withheld, and the poor and widows were being mistreated. This was not a new problem.

When we think about our racialized society from very early on in the history of the United States (and beyond), the institutions of our society have been likewise culpable of systemic sin; every institution (because we live in a fallen world) is subject to it. For those who take the Bible seriously, this should not come as a surprise. Whether an institution is political, religious, economic, or related to law enforcement, it has the potential to establish systems that work against the good of humanity, whether intended or not. Every institution has the unfortunate capacity to give advantage to some and disadvantage to others, to bring privilege to some and pain to others.

As you take in all this, you might be overwhelmed, but stay with me. To work through these issues requires us to take the time needed to grasp them. But it's worth it because our world needs deeply formed people in this arena. Before I present a number of practical ways forward, I want to close this chapter by highlighting four misunderstandings about racial reconciliation.

We Assume That Racial Reconciliation Is Possible Without Justice

There can be no true reconciliation without justice. For relationships to be fully restored, things have to be made right. Justice is the presence of right verdicts and right relationships, and it's characterized by undoing power abuses and redressing sins against oppressed people.

> There can be no true reconciliation without
> justice.

Many who sincerely yearn for reconciliation can want to merely name the sins of the past, wash one another's feet, and then just move on without further thought or action toward justice. While these gestures may be beautifully moving, the larger systemic social injustices continue unhindered, creating fragmented relationships and ruined lives.

It should also be noted that working for justice should not be restricted only to taking up one's cause with those in political power (as necessary an act as that often is). The pursuit of justice more often is about taking up one's cause with whoever is in power in whatever context and seeking to work collaboratively to bring about fairness, just policies, and equitable community life.

We Assume That Racial Reconciliation Means Color Blindness

For many people, color blindness is seen as a virtue—something to be applauded and celebrated. Some people are still fond of saying, "I don't see color; I see people." And although that seems really sweet, color blindness is not the MO of heaven: "I looked, and behold, a great multitude that no one could number, from every nation, from all tribes and peoples and languages, standing before the throne and before the Lamb" (Revelation 7:9). God sees all the color.

To be sure, when many people speak of being color-blind, their intentions are good. The focus of the color-blind model is that no one should enjoy any economic or social advantages based on skin color. But in the end, the language of color blindness is the attempt to establish relationship by denying diversity and our honest differences. So as good as intentions may be, pretending to be color-blind is still playing at something other than the truth.

We Equate Diversity with Racial Reconciliation

To be sure, diversity is a good thing, but in and of itself, it is not the same as reconciliation. On the surface, diversity looks wonderful, especially in church settings. However, as with justice, the temptation is for us to stop there. When we make diversity the end goal, we are no different from New York City subway cars. New York City subway cars are crowds of diverse, anonymous people in close proximity. But the church is called to be more than a sanctified subway car.

When the gospel is deeply at work, racial reconciliation results in a diverse community that embraces the unique gifts and acknowledges the distinctive sins of their ethnic-racial-social makeup while experiencing loving communion with others under the lordship of Jesus.

We Want Friendship or Evangelism to Solve Racism

The common response to addressing the institutional underpinnings of racism or the individual racial prejudice we carry is often cloaked in language of strategic warm-and-fuzzy interpersonal relationships. This is especially true in much of the evangelical culture. There are two particularly relevant strategies highlighted by Michael Emerson and Christian Smith in their seminal book, *Di-*

vided by Faith.[10] Emerson and Smith noted that the classic strategies taken up by evangelicals are those of conversion and friendship.

Believers often think that if we can only convert more people to Christianity, this will solve the issue of racism. We think that if someone makes a decision for Jesus, this will end his or her racialized perspectives. So the goal becomes to just bring into the Christian fold as many of those diverse people as possible. But history has shown that some of the worst racist behavior has come from within the Christian fold.

The other approach is the interpersonal friendship strategy, with the rationale being, "If only we had enough friendships with people from other races, this would solve everything. If we simply had more skills and training to relate to each other better, racism would be overcome." But that's only one part of the issue. While both of these purposes (evangelism and friendship) are incredibly important, navigating our racialized society requires a multifaceted approach, which I will take us through in the next chapter.

FOUR

Deeply Formed Practices of Racial Reconciliation

In 2019, one month after our church's annual Gospel and Race conference, a small group of Black congregants asked for a private meeting with me. I thought the conference was a success, so I wondered what the meeting could be about. For the conference, we brought in top-notch thinkers and leaders from the outside, but it was evident to some in our church that we still had lots of work to do on the inside.

For three decades, our congregation has worked extremely hard to bridge racial barriers. Our staff, leadership, preachers, and worship leaders represent the diversity of our congregation. We address racial injustice, encourage relationships across ethnic differences, and seek to model something of the kingdom of God. But even with this history, there remain blind spots.

In the days preceding the meeting, I heard words of frustration from some of the people who were planning on attending, so I was already on guard. When the time came, we sat at a round table in one of the church meeting spaces.

I walked in and greeted the ten congregants who were already patiently waiting for our time to begin. I did my pastoral thing, greeting everyone around the table. There were genuine smiles, hugs, and handshakes exchanged, yet I sensed some tension in the room. Three other pastors joined me in the meeting to listen to the perspectives of these congregants. I had a piece of paper handy so I could take notes and a cup of water to hide behind in the event that things got too tense. It didn't take long for the points of tension to be expressed. Each person took a turn first affirming the work we've done over the years and then proceeding to share any frustrations.

The things I heard made my heart sink: "Pastor, I feel invisible." "I don't know if I belong here." "I wonder when things will change." "When will we get equal treatment here?" "We've made progress, Pastor Rich, but we have a long way to go." The main frustration was that some ethnic groups had the blessing and support of church leadership to gather and meet, but other ethnic groups were not afforded that support. There was some hard truth in their observations. The meeting continued, and others told of the hurt they felt because of racial insensitivity in regular conversations at church and what they observed on social media from other congregants.

As I listened, I captured the comments on paper, which gave me a bit of emotional distance from the surprising and disorienting words I hadn't expected. I have worked hard to preach and lead from a place of racial justice and reconciliation, but it was evident that some people in our congregation still felt the scars of our racialized world. How could this be?

This meeting led to additional good conversations,

which helped us pinpoint particular areas that needed to be discerned, such as whether we needed more ethnic-specific communities within our church, and it served as a good reminder that the work of racial healing is deep. Our leadership team agreed that we were not equipping leaders at our church well enough to promote our core value of reconciliation, so we decided to gather together key leaders to dialogue, train, and deepen our commitment to racial wholeness. For us, the journey continues.

RACIAL HABITS

A multifaceted problem requires a multifaceted solution. It requires us to establish a new set of racial habits (or disciplines) to deeply form us. In his book *Democracy in Black,* professor Eddie Glaude wrote, "Everyone possesses racial habits, often without even realizing it. Habits, in general, predispose us to see our world in particular ways, and often we consider them helpful things. . . . Not only do these habits shape how we interact with people of different racial backgrounds, they also guide how we think about and value groups collectively."[1]

We all have racial habits. We all have conscious and unconscious ways of racially engaging others. Some habits are rooted in love, justice, and appreciation for others' differences; other habits are rooted in ignorance, fear, and a propensity to marginalize whoever is different. But the good news is that bad habits can be changed. For old habits to die, we need a new set of habits in their places. What does a deeply formed life look like when offering racial healing and justice? I propose seven habits.

THE HABIT OF REMEMBERING

You can't understand the current experience of racial hostility, especially in the United States, without also honestly facing the racial discrimination that's taken place throughout history, including racial oppression experienced by Native Americans and slavery experienced by African Americans. As a pastor of a very diverse church, I'm aware of the racial prejudice and racism that takes place all over the world. Every country in the world has some measure of racial hostility and tension, but I want to focus particularly on life in the United States.

The divisiveness and racial injustice we are experiencing today is the fruit of centuries of racial oppression and hostility. People often want to look to the success of individual minorities as proof that racial oppression has been eradicated, but that's much too simplistic a view. James Baldwin aptly pointed out, "The inequalities suffered by the many are in no way justified by the rise of a few."[2] The residue of racial inequality and hostility remains. On a personal level, we can't understand our present reality without an honest recognition of our past. The same principle applies to our present national reality.

At New Life, we have a spiritual formation tool we use called the *genogram* (more on this in chapter 6). A genogram is a tool out of family systems theory for examining the ways we have been shaped by our families of origin. It reveals both the positive and negative legacies that have been handed down. Unless we look back to see how we have been improperly formed, we will continue to live out the same patterns from one generation to the next. This tool has broader use, as it applies to our churches and country as well. The goal of doing a genogram as an individual is not to hate your parents and families; it's to objectively assess the good, the bad, and the ugly. The same applies for our country: to look at the history of our country is not to result in us hating it; in all actuality, it's to help us love it better.

Unless we look back to see how we have been improperly formed, we will continue to live out the same patterns from one generation to the next.

In bringing up history, it's important to say that just like human beings, the United States is a mix. It's not all bad, and it's not all good. I'm grateful to live in the United States, and I'm not blind to the ways this country has fallen short over and over again. I know that for some people, to even confess this seems a mark of ungratefulness. For some, to speak about our country's dark past is just not acceptable. I've heard many say, "If you don't love this country, leave." But that's much oversimplified and spiritually dangerous. Our refusal to honestly look at the dark history of the United States often reveals an idolatry of the heart.

Author and lawyer Bryan Stevenson described an American "narrative of racial difference" that was an enduring and dangerous myth plaguing much of its people's collective consciousness: "The great evil of American slavery was not involuntary servitude and forced labor.

To me, the great evil of slavery was the narrative of racial difference, the ideology of white supremacy that we created to make ourselves feel comfortable with enslaving people who are black. We've never addressed that legacy."[3]

This narrative is more than just recognizing differences of race. The problem is that differences are assigned value and worth. In other words, the sin is in the hierarchy that was created based on racial differences. This hierarchy has served as the impetus for lynching, segregation, myriad civil rights abuses, and the ever-present "othering" that often leads to violence.

I appreciate that for some this kind of language comes across as scapegoating and finger-pointing. I've had many good-hearted White brothers and sisters say to me, "I've never owned slaves" or "I would never treat anyone like people did in the past." I understand their frustration. No one wants to be categorized by some of the most racist and evil deeds in American history. At the same time, to imply that the residue of racism is nonexistent is to turn our eyes away from that which is painfully obvious to many. The purpose of honestly wrestling with history is to see where we have been and how we are still being formed by the myths, narratives, and practices of the past.

In the Bible, one of the most-repeated words is *remember*. God had to consistently remind his people where they came from, lest they repeat the sins of their past. As we remember together, we are positioned to learn from history and not repeat it.

Let me try to explain this need to look back through another lens: through the analogy of sexism. Sexism, like racism, has been around for a long time. Men have lived with a social advantage over women for millennia, which has led to unjust policies, systems, practices, and assumptions. Take a quick look at who is in power in our world. Who is calling the shots? Who is oppressing others? It's men. Now, I can work hard to be anti-sexist, but if I don't painstakingly sit with the truth that I have been a beneficiary of a society that privileges men over women, I'm not going to help move the conversation in the best direction.

I learned this lesson from George Yancy, professor of philosophy at Emory University. He is the author of *Backlash: What Happens When We Talk Honestly About Racism in America*. Prior to the release of the book, Yancy wrote a *New York Times* op-ed piece titled "Dear White America." He wanted to underscore the ongoing racial situation and the ways White people benefit from racism. The article received a jarring backlash from White readers. What I found particularly helpful and illuminating was his ability to clearly name the sexism that he benefits from. Here's a short excerpt:

> What if I told you that I'm sexist? . . .
>
> This doesn't mean that I intentionally hate women or that I desire to oppress them. It means that despite my best intentions, I perpetuate sexism every day of my life. . . .
>
> As a sexist, I have failed women. I have failed to speak out when I should have. I have failed to engage critically and extensively their pain and suffering in my writing. I have failed to

transcend the rigidity of gender roles in my own life. I have failed to challenge those poisonous assumptions that women are "inferior" to men or to speak out loudly in the company of male philosophers who believe that feminist philosophy is just a non-philosophical fad. I have been complicit with, and have allowed myself to be seduced by, a country that makes billions of dollars from sexually objectifying women, from pornography, commercials, video games, to Hollywood movies. I am not innocent.[4]

I join Yancy in this confession, as I, too, am not innocent. And how can we make progress in the conversation on sexism if we refuse to take seriously the historical reality that brought us to this place? Likewise, how can we make progress in the conversation on racism if we refuse to take seriously the historical reality?

THE HABIT OF INCARNATIONAL LISTENING

Also crucial to the deeply formed life is a deep commitment to listening to others even when it's hard. When it comes to conversations on race, our level of offendability often reveals the level of our maturity. If we can't overcome offense in the moment, we are not going to get very far. Reconciliation requires us to listen deeply to one another. In the following chapter on interior examination, I will explore this further, but for now I want to highlight this great need we all must grow into.

> When it comes to conversations on race, our level of offendability often reveals the level of our maturity.

To some degree, most of us can admit that we can do better at listening, yet this remains virtually impossible for many reasons. For example, we equate listening to agreement, we would rather be right than open our minds to different perspectives, we might carry deep anxiety about negotiating differences, we reduce people to their worst belief, or we are simply afraid of change.

When I look at my life, I can see these perspectives flowing through me. As a result, listening is hard. Why? Well, to truly listen to another person requires something of a crucifixion. I must undergo a painful process of leaving what is familiar territory (my perspective on the matter) and make space in my heart for a different narrative.

At New Life, any strategy to racial healing in our neighborhoods requires us to practice incarnational listening. Like Jesus's movement from Word to flesh, incarnational listening requires three movements of the heart.[5]

1. *Leave your world.* Let go of the familiar, take the risk, and step out (especially with regard to race and culture).

2. *Enter into someone else's world.* Practice active, humble, and curious listening.

3. *Allow yourself to be formed by others.* Open up to their worldviews while holding on to yourself.

In this way, incarnation describes not only Jesus's ministry to us but also how we can minister by listening to one another.

We have a congregant named Isaac Lee Chung who directed a film called *Munyurangabo*.[6] It tells the story of a young man seeking to make sense of his life after the Rwandan genocide. He wants to exact revenge on the man who killed his father, so he travels with a machete, bent on vengeance. By the end of the story, something surprising occurs: a glimmer of reconciliation. Chung interestingly described how, through the film's production, he himself came to understand about the process of reconciliation:

> Reconciliation involves a willing act to be vulnerable to another culture, and I found that this can't be authentic if it's done with any feeling that the other culture is better or worse than your own. When I went to Rwanda, I thought that as a Korean who grew up on a farm in Arkansas, I knew a lot about bridging cultures. But I realized I had some deep-seated prejudices in assuming that I had more to offer people in Rwanda than they had to offer me. It would have been just as false to assume that I had nothing to offer, demonizing my Western and Eastern upbringing to embrace a fully African way of life.
>
> Instead, when I embraced them as equals and they saw me in the same way, I have seen us shape each other in a healthy way, as good friends. I also found that there was never a mo-

ment of epiphany that made me embrace and learn from Rwandan culture. Instead, every conversation and visit seemed like a process, the way close family members might have issues they must work through for an entire lifetime. This still isn't easy for me, and it doesn't come naturally. But my commitment to the friendships I have in Rwanda is a commitment to keep at the process of reconciliation, believing that deep down, this process itself is holy work.[7]

This is the work of reconciliation—not that we despise ourselves or others but that we listen and live humbly and incarnationally and through that process see the image of God in one another. Reconciliation is hard and protracted work, yet by the grace of God and the courageous steps we take, we can begin to taste today what is waiting for us when the new creation is fully consummated.

While we are all called to listen to one another in the bond of peace, the ones who need to listen first and more often are those who have enjoyed the privileges of social power. This is a deeply Christ-centered way of being. The one who has power or has benefited from the ways power has socially arranged his or her world must be called upon to lead the way in listening. For the same reason, men must lead the way in listening first and more often to women, as they have thoroughly held power and have enjoyed the benefits of a world ordered by patriarchy. So too must wealthy, upwardly mobile men and women listen first and more often to the experiences of poor and working-class people. They have enjoyed the benefits of wealth and power and are often far removed from the plights of the poor.

It is along these same lines that our White brothers and sisters need to lead in listening deeply to the stories and experiences of people of color and listening more often. The social construct of race that this fallen world has created, broadly speaking, has normalized and rendered superior White people. This reality doesn't mean people of color don't need to listen (we certainly do), but order is important. To be an incarnational follower of Christ, there must be a relinquishing of control, a reversal of social order. According to the natural perceptions of this world, it's an upside-down kingdom. But it's a kingdom of God-saturated imagination. It's the way of the Cross.

THE HABIT OF LAMENT

Deeply formed reconciliation can't happen without the spiritual discipline of lamenting. The act of lament is the spiritually mature response to sadness and sorrow. Theology professor Soong-Chan Rah insisted, "Lament recognizes the struggles of life and cries out for justice against existing injustices."[8] In the practice of lamenting, we pour out our souls to God and in turn receive grace and power to respond.

Lamenting is an act that helps facilitate personal wholeness and public rightness, and when we practice it, we have solid biblical ground to stand on. At least one-third of the book of Psalms are songs of lament. Within these biblical songs, we are given a divine model for cultivating a spirituality of grief and the social grace that is offered by God as a result. Psalms offer us language to access our souls for the purpose of working for a better world.

The sad truth about modern spirituality is that we often avoid feeling our own pain and in the process avoid feeling the pain of others. When this happens, it's impossible to do the work of reconciliation. For good reason, Paul calls us to weep with those who weep (see Romans 12:15). Beyond the personal blessing of comfort for those who mourn, it is often our tears that serve as the foundation for spiritual transformation and for a new social imagination. The act of lamenting often results in prophetic vision to deeply name the powers that work against reconciliation. To lament is not simply to cry out but also to discern God's direction through the tears.

It's especially important to understand that lamenting goes far deeper than our current culture of moral outrage. In our day, the work of justice and reconciliation has been substituted by short-lived anger that is easily distracted, tears that start and end with tweets, and fiery rants that avoid any clear sense of action. A culture of moral outrage often results in greater antagonism being created because the end result is not *shalom* ("peace") but self-serving catharsis.

Lament, on the other hand, is a fueling of action motivated by compassion rather than catharsis. It requires us to take seriously the pain we see and feel and to open ourselves to how God might have us respond. This can especially happen as we gather in worship with others during times of social unrest. There have been times when I've gathered with friends or a congregation to prayerfully name the pain, injustice, and grief that the world was experiencing. In those moments, the suffering and anger were not swept under the carpet of religious denial. Rather, as the pain was named, I would see people emerge with new vision to be witnesses of God's reconciling power.

THE HABIT OF RECONCILING PRAYER

The racial hostility in our world is so deep that we would be mistaken to think we can make significant progress without the depth of spirituality in prayer. There are principalities and powers at work in the world; therefore, the church is in desperate need of reimagining prayer both in personal and congregational environments. As a pastor, I'm most concerned about the lack of time that people give to prayer. This lack of prayer has marked the lives of the modern church as practicing, in the words of Parker Palmer, "functional atheism."[9]

The gospel of Mark recounts Jesus's explanation to his disciples for their inability to handle a demon he'd just cast out: "This kind cannot be driven out by anything but prayer" (9:29). When it comes to the evil power of racism and the racialized world we live in, the same principle applies. It's noteworthy that the profound work undertaken by Martin Luther King Jr. and those in the civil rights movement was undergirded by prayer. In an important article, King's wife, Coretta, wrote, "Prayer was a wellspring of strength and inspiration during the Civil Rights Movement. Throughout the movement, we prayed for greater human understanding. We prayed for the safety of our compatriots in the freedom struggle. We prayed for victory in our nonviolent protests, for brotherhood and sisterhood among people of all races, for reconciliation and the fulfillment of the Beloved Community."[10]

A deep life with God is required when engaging the powers of racial hostility, because in our work to dismantle this power, we can be prone to using tactics that conform to the destructive ways of this world. A person working for racial justice and reconciliation without a deep spirituality of prayer is missing an important part of the healing process.

This is why the image of the redwood root system I alluded to in the introduction is such a helpful analogy. I've seen many people work for racial justice and reconciliation without any commitment to prayer. When we live this way, we only see ourselves as righteous heroes exposing the powers of the world, while not seeing how complicit we are as parts of the world's sinful structures. Prayer forges humility and opens us up to the love of God, out of which we work for healing. In this respect, prayer is both formational and invitational. Prayer forms us into people marked by the fruit of the Spirit; in prayer we invite God into the struggle of our lives.

In our work of reconciliation, prayer is a steadfast refusal to give ourselves over to either resignation or self-reliance. Resignation says that things will never change. Self-reliance says we can change things in our own strength. The former is marked by despair, the latter by a futile confidence in our own efforts. Prayer for reconciliation's sake is not disengaged and removed from the realities of life. Prayer can infuse us with, in the words of Old Testament theologian Walter Brueggemann, a "prophetic imagination."[11]

> In our work of reconciliation, prayer is a steadfast refusal to give ourselves over to either resignation or self-reliance.

In 2017, Charlottesville, Virginia, was caught in the national spotlight. A White supremacist rally, fueled by the removal of Confederate monuments across the South, led to counterprotests and violence. That weekend, an Ohio man plowed his car through the crowd of counter-protesters, killing a thirty-two-year-old woman who was walking down the street. As I watched the news unfold on TV, I was profoundly grieved by the overt spectacle of unending racial fragmentation and was moved to craft a prayer for our church to offer God together. The Sunday following the terrible event, we prayed this together at our worship services:

> Lord Jesus, your kingdom is good news for a world caught in racial hostility. We ask that you give us grace for the deep challenges our country faces.
>
> We confess our anger, our deep sadness, and our collective sense of weakness to see this world healed through our own strength.
>
> We honestly confess that our country has a long history of racial oppression; that racism

has been a strategy of evil powers and principalities infected by structural sin.

We confess that the gospel is good news for the oppressed and the oppressor. Both are raised up; both are liberated but in different ways. The oppressed are raised up from the harsh burden of inferiority, the oppressor from the destructive illusion of superiority.

We confess that the gospel is your power to form a new people not identified by dominance and superiority but by unity in the Spirit.

We ask that you help us name our part in this country's story of racial oppression and hostility. Whether we have sinned against others by seeing them as inferior or have been silent in the face of evil, forgive us of our sin.

We pray for our enemies—for those who have allowed satanic powers to work through them. Grant them deliverance through your mighty power.

We ask that you form us to be peacemakers. May we be people who speak the truth in love as we work for a reconciled world.

Lord, we commit our lives to you, believing that you are working in the world in spite of destructive powers and principalities. Bring healing to those who are hurt, peace to those who are anxious, and love to those who are fearful. We wait for you, Lord. Make haste to help us.

Oh, Lord, only you can make all things new.

Everything wasn't magically healed in that moment, but I believe that the Spirit was deeply at work in us as we confessed our powerlessness to God. A handful of people approached me with a renewed vision to connect prayer with their activism. They saw that prayer was not a way to ignore the problem but rather a means of engaging the issues from a different place—a deeper place. Unless people are instructed to have lives with God in prayer, any hope to see deep racial reconciliation literally won't have a prayer.

THE HABIT OF RACIAL SELF-EXAMINATION

One of the ways we dishonor the image of God in others is by not doing the hard work of examining the assumptions and biases we have against them. We have all been socialized by our families of origin and surrounding culture to see people in particular ways. We often live our lives without ever reflecting on the stories and lies we've been told about certain groups of people. Consequently, we perpetuate the myths and stereotypes subconsciously. Racial reconciliation requires us to have a level of self-awareness that often is tragically missing in our culture.

A few years ago, I was in a library in Queens working on a sermon. While deep in thought, I glanced to the left and saw a Black man slowly looking around the library. My initial thought was a question: *What is he looking for?* The question very quickly became an assumption (*he's looking to steal something*) morphed into a judgment. In the twenty seconds that all this took place, I soon discovered—to my shame—that the man was looking for a place to charge his phone. In a New York minute, I went from observing to interpreting to judging. Something deep was at work in me. Similarly, on several occasions, I have been on an airplane when a man who looks possibly Middle Eastern has walked to the front of the plane to use the bathroom. I'm sad to confess that I've jumped to conclusions about him. I actually have wondered, *Why is he taking so long in there?* Assumptions are effortlessly made. Something deep is at work in me.

My wife and I moved into an apartment building in a marginally diverse neighborhood. Our brown skin stands out in this neighborhood. On the day before we moved in, my wife took cleaning supplies to our apartment to sweep and mop before the furniture was transported in. As my wife left carrying the bucket and mop, a well-meaning White woman chased her down, asking, "Excuse me, are you the cleaning lady? I'm looking for someone to hire." When my wife firmly let her know that we were moving in, the woman was absolutely mortified. She saw a short Latina with cleaning supplies in hand and thought that she certainly couldn't live *there*. Something deep was at work in that woman.

As previously mentioned, implicit racial prejudice infects all of us, but we need not passively acquiesce to it. The habit of racial self-examination shapes us into people who don't look at the outward appearance. This short list of questions might help you identify any subconscious perspectives you have of others:

- Is there a particular people, ethnicity, or race that you don't trust? Why?

- Is there any particular people, ethnicity, or race that you or your child cannot marry? Why?

- What types of people cause you to cross the street if you are walking alone? Why?

- What, if anything, happens inside you when you see interracial couples? Why?

- When was the last time you visited the residence of someone from a different culture or race, or invited the person to your residence?

- What type of person would you most trust to invest or steward your money? Why?

As we honestly respond to these questions, the internal scripts and messages that we have lived with can be met with alternative messages. This is deeply formed work. It's not easy, but as we identify the ways we've been deeply de-formed in our thinking toward others, we position ourselves to walk in greater freedom.

THE HABIT OF RENOUNCING WHITENESS

In one of my sermons on race, I attempted to make a distinction between White people and Whiteness. The former speaks to human beings made in the image of God; the latter speaks to a destructive ideology that normalizes and absolutizes so-called White values, experiences, and history. My failed attempt at this distinction brought about anger from people in my congregation. Some had difficulty separating the two, accusing me of reverse racism. But deeply formed reconciliation requires us to do the hard work of clarifying and distinguishing between these two ideas.

Truthfully, no one is born White. Whiteness—like race in general—is a human creation that was established to create a hierarchy of human value. Whiteness is a lens one sees through to determine such things as validity, safety, and normalcy. In the words of American theologian Willie James Jennings, "Whiteness was . . . a way of organizing bodies by proximity to and approximation of white bodies."[12] Said another way, Whiteness is an absolute way of viewing and assigning value to the world through the racialized perspective of White normativity.

There was a time in history when "White people" did not exist, meaning they were known and identified exclusively by their ethnic, national identity. They identified as Italian, Irish, British, or German, and before that as Celts, Scythians, Vikings, or Anglo-Saxons. But over time, as the European empires that grew from these ethnic groups came into contact with people who didn't look like them, they felt an unfortunate need to classify, distinguish, and rank.

In his book *White Awake,* Daniel Hill highlights the analysis of British sociologist Alastair Bonnett, who said that "there was something unique about white culture, especially when observed in relation to nonwhite cultures: in both countries [United States and Britain] white culture is the 'norm' by which all other cultural identities are evaluated."[13]

Let me give some examples of this. Whiteness is at work when:

- certain neighborhoods are deemed *inherently* better when White people are present, and inferior when they are not;

- skin color is viewed as *inherently* superior the lighter it is;

- certain hair types are viewed as *inherently* good while some are seen as inferior; and

- white people are inherently seen as more reliable, authoritative, and trustworthy than people of color.

Some might argue that if we are called to renounce Whiteness, why not do the same with Blackness and Brownness? It's a good question, but the distinction is massive. Whiteness has historically been a force of oppression (slavery, Jim Crow laws, discrimination, apartheid, and so on), rendering other people as inferior and even subhuman. Historically speaking, retaining Blackness or Brownness had been an act of survival and a heightening of dignity. For example, when Black men and women have proclaimed "Black is beautiful," it's an affirmation of value in a world that has regarded Black as ugly or inferior.

So, then, what does it mean to renounce Whiteness? For people identified as White or otherwise, it simply means acknowledging the lens. For many years, I grew up believing that I would "make it" if I moved into a White neighborhood. I thought that would validate my existence. I would prove to others that I was somebody. To renounce Whiteness, in this case, is to do the hard work of rooting my identity in God's love *and* repenting of the ways I have assigned (or not assigned) value to entire groups of people. It's a lifelong work of rejecting the often-internalized hierarchy that shapes how we view ourselves and others. Ironically, one can be Latinx or Asian and be deeply formed by Whiteness. On the other hand, one can be White but regularly reject and turn from Whiteness as a lens through which one sees the world. It's complicated.

THE HABIT OF REGULAR CONFESSION, REPENTANCE, AND FORGIVENESS

Finally, reconciliation requires regular confession, repentance, and forgiveness. We come together as deeply broken and frail people. At our church, when we gather for communion, we recite a historic confession from the *Book of Common Prayer.* This confession anchors us as people in desperate need of regular repentance and forgiveness. I submit this as a confession we regularly repeat as we work for racial reconciliation:

> Most merciful God,
> we confess that we have sinned against you
> in thought, word, and deed,
> by what we have done,
> and by what we have left undone.
> We have not loved you with our whole heart;
> we have not loved our neighbors as ourselves.
> We are truly sorry and we humbly repent.
> For the sake of your Son Jesus Christ,

have mercy on us and forgive us;
that we may delight in your will,
and walk in your ways,
to the glory of your Name. Amen.[14]

Let's face it: we sin against God, and we sin against each other. We are all complicit. Croatian theologian Miroslav Volf has said, "Forgiveness flounders because I exclude the enemy from the community of humans even as I exclude myself from the community of sinners."[15] Christians are called to the deeply formed ways of confession, repentance, and forgiveness.

To be deeply formed for racial reconciliation means we must open ourselves to the truth that things we hate in others we also find in ourselves. In confession and repentance, we see that we have disappointed people, dominated and used others to their harm, rarely if ever given away power unless forced to, said harsh things, not followed through on a promise, gossiped, lied, been insensitive, and been unforgiving. We have confessed to being followers of Jesus without becoming truly shaped by the values he lived and died for. We have, in fact, applied our religion in ways that benefit ourselves but bring harm to millions.

Now, this doesn't mean we do away with justice or consequences; rather, first we begin with looking at how we are in many ways no different from the people we dislike. God wants to form the world deeply for the work of healing, and this kind of forming requires interior examination.

FIVE

Interior Examination for a World Living on the Surface

I know what it's like to live a divided life. When I joined New Life Fellowship Church as an assistant pastor, I was twenty-nine years old. By that time, I had lots of experience separating my inner life from my outer one. I had difficulty being honest with others about my anger and sadness, especially with my wife and people in the church. As a result, everyone loved me. The question was, Were they loving the true Rich?

Rosie and I had been married for almost three years. We communicated well and certainly had our share of disagreements and arguments, but I continuously had a hard time being fully vulnerable with her about the things that bothered me. On a regular basis, she would ask if I was upset, but I would routinely respond, "No, I'm frustrated." Frustrated seemed like a more Christian response than anger.

In all this, however, Rosie was (and remains) much too perceptive to let that kind of response slide. In a moment of calm, she would say to me, "I'm really scared that one day you're just going to snap. One day you're going to explode, and I'm afraid what you might do." She found out one day.

Throughout my childhood, I carried a lot of anger. I'm sure growing up in a rough Brooklyn neighborhood contributed to it. Anger is commonly the only way to survive in those environments. My anger was often my defense mechanism, shielding me from the deeper anxiety I felt. In my case, however, I carried it but didn't communicate it.

In any event, Rosie and I were in the middle of an argument, and the conversation took us from the living room to the kitchen (a good ten feet in our small Queens apartment). She is an external processor, meaning she thinks and talks everything out loud. And for many unhealthy reasons, I would not respond to the moment with my own words on the matter.

So what was happening here? I'm a preacher. I know how to communicate. I know how to string words together in ways that connect with people. Yet in my most important relationship, words have often failed me. I have had to learn how to speak from a different place in my soul to connect with my wife. Preaching from a pulpit is one thing; communicating in the kitchen is quite another.

I don't even recall what Rosie and I were arguing about, but I felt powerless to unanxiously remain present, and this feeling produced a mounting surge of anger on the inside. I didn't have the tools to access my anger or my sadness in a way that would bring me close to Rosie. As she shared her frustrations about the matter, I welled up on the inside. As my body tensed, I began to mentally check out.

I had my iPhone in hand, and in a moment of rage, I

violently slammed it on the marble kitchen table, shattering the screen. It was the first time I had expressed that level of anger before her. I then stormed out of the apartment and took a long walk around the neighborhood to try to cool down. After an hour of stewing in my anger, I knew I couldn't continue living that way. First of all, fixing that phone was expensive. More importantly, I was divided.

In Swiss psychologist Alice Miller's provocative book *The Body Never Lies,* she named the tragic reality experienced by people who cut themselves off from their feelings and compensate this loss by appealing to the often sterile, unfeeling institution of the church:

> People who have been severed from their true feelings since early childhood will be dependent on institutions like the church and will let themselves be told what they are allowed to feel. In most cases it is very little indeed. But I cannot imagine that it will always be like this. Somewhere, sometime, there will be a rebellion, and the process of mutual stultification will be halted. It will be halted when individuals summon up the courage to overcome their understandable fears, to tell, feel, and publish the truth and communicate with others on this basis.[1]

Miller's vision for a rebellion isn't argued from a Christian perspective, but I believe that her words capture the essence of what faith in Jesus entails. To follow Jesus in this world requires us to embrace a fully human life, alive to the dimensions of our interior worlds that often are repressed, ignored, and explained away with Bible verses and in the name of respectability. A rebellion is indeed needed—a rebellion marked by truth, integrity, and wholeness. That's what I'd like to lead us into through this chapter.

A rebellion is indeed needed—a rebellion
marked by truth, integrity, and wholeness.

In a less demonstrative moment, I found myself divided yet again. This time it was at church. A year or so after joining New Life as a pastor, I was given an opportunity to preach at our Good Friday services. Many people would be coming to church to remember what Christ had done for them on the cross. We set up contemplative-prayer centers around the building, prominently displayed a large wooden cross, and created what felt like a very sacred environment.

I prepared my PowerPoint presentation with care, not looking to overwhelm the congregation with points and content but with powerful images that complemented the preached Word. Before the first of two services, I stopped by the audiovisual booth to ensure that my slides were ready to go. The person at the booth gave me a thumbs-up. When it was time for me to speak, I stepped onto the platform and began preaching. I sensed the congregation was with me. My sermon was going well, and I was ready to land the final truth using an image that would certainly remain etched in their minds for years to come.

When it was time for the unveiling of that image on the screen, I asked the volunteer to advance the slide, but in that moment all I could see was a bright blank blue screen. Because it was dark in the room, the bright light was hard on the eyes. I again asked her to advance it, to no avail. I was a bit disoriented but finished the message. I was disappointed the congregation didn't get to see the image, but I found solace in the fact that we had two services. Thank God! I walked back to the AV booth and asked the volunteer what had happened. She said she didn't know but would make sure everything was fixed for the second service and gave another thumbs-up. I walked away assured that what happened in the first service was a strange aberration.

When it was time for my part again, I stepped onto the platform and began preaching. I again felt that the congregation was with me and I was setting the stage to bring forth that powerful image. I prepped the scene and, gesturing to the AV volunteer, said, "Please advance the slide." I confidently looked up, preparing for the collective congregational "wow," but once again, all I could see was a godforsaken bright blank blue screen. Just two minutes ago, I was preaching about the love found in the cross. Two minutes later, I was thinking about putting that volunteer on that prominently displayed cross in the sanctuary.

I closed my sermon with a word of prayer and dismissed the congregation to the prayer centers around the building. On the inside, I was fuming. I walked to the AV booth, and the volunteer nonchalantly said, "Sorry about that, Rich."

I responded with my divided self by saying, "No worries." I didn't express any anger or disappointment, but I carried tons of resentment.

A couple of weeks later, New Life founding pastor Pete Scazzero called me into his office. He mentioned that the Emotionally Healthy Leadership conference was soon approaching and he was hoping I could participate in some way. He wanted to have me practice an emotionally healthy skill called Climb the Ladder of Integrity. Basically, my task would be to honestly communicate to another staff member (in front of three hundred leaders) an area where a personal value had been violated. He asked me if I was angry at anyone since coming on staff.

I thought for just a second and said, "Nope." I let him know that all had been good and that I had no complaints.

With a bit of a side-eye, Pete asked, "Are you sure?"

I thought again and my mind flashed back to the image in my head of that volunteer suffering on the cross as a result of messing up my sermon. I told Pete about Good Friday and my anger with the volunteer but more so my anger with the worship pastor who assigned her that role. Pete seemed a bit too pleased to hear about my distress and asked me if I would share about it. I agreed to go through the exercise.

By God's grace, I survived. The worship pastor received my words with grace and maturity, but I'm frightened to think about the damage my soul would have had to endure and the falseness of my relationship with other staff members had I not been invited to look within.

Sadly, this is the standard way of life in our churches, families, and workplaces. What I was being invited into was a life of interior examination for the sake of loving well. Without it, a deeply formed life is impossible.

INTERIOR EXAMINATION AS A WAY OF LIFE

Interior examination is a way of life that considers the realities of our inner worlds for the sake of our own flourishing and the call to love well. Yet much of modern life resists this kind of living. As theologian Ronald Rolheiser warned, "The air we breathe today is generally not conducive to interiority and depth."[2] We live on the tip of the iceberg, and for various reasons. Many of our days are strategically and subconsciously constructed to avoid looking beneath the surface. We often belong to church communities that reinforce a lack of introspection. We use God to run from God, and we use God to run from ourselves. It's so easy to do this.

Interior examination is a way of life that considers the realities of our inner worlds for the sake of our own flourishing and the call to love well.

Beyond our personal lives and church communities, our entire world is oriented against interior examination. There is often a paralyzing fear and a compartmentalized approach to life that reinforces our lack of inner investigation. But after a while it catches up. I'm reminded of my experience with my first car.

I've never been one to work with my hands fixing things. I spent most of my childhood playing sports and most of my adulthood reading, writing, and speaking. So when I purchased my first car, I rarely looked under the hood. I infrequently went to the mechanic to get oil changes. I never rotated my tires or checked my car fluids. I turned the car on, drove, parked, and repeated the process. But over time, a dangerous kind of wear and tear was lurking.

On one occasion as a college student, I was driving around the campus and heard a strange thumping sound. As the weekend progressed, the sound got louder and more frequent. After a couple of days of hearing these troubling noises, I decided to do what any person who has no time or skill to address these issues does: I put down the windows and blasted the music. *Ah, so much better.*

The next day, as I drove to my grandmother's home in Brooklyn with some friends in the car, my tire exploded on the highway. Boom! Thankfully, no one was driving near us on the highway, but it was a terrifying lesson I learned very quickly. Sooner or later the stuff we ignore will explode when we least expect it.

Looking under the hood of our souls or at the lower deck of our lives or beneath the surface of the iceberg requires something of us. That is why I love the book of Psalms. It has been a guide and model of interior examination for me.

THE BOOK OF PSALMS AS A MODEL OF INTERIOR EXAMINATION

The book of Psalms is filled with words of worship to God, but it is also filled with the language of interior searching and examination. If you spend any amount of time reading Psalms, you'll find out quickly that these songs are not nursery rhymes; they are raw, authentic, honest songs that capture the emotional spectrum of the psalmist's life. You'll see words of grief, of anger and rage, of fear and anxiety, and of joy, hope, and worship.

So if this is the prayer book of the people of God, these words are to become our words. These words are not just for singing and reading; they are for giving expression to what's happening inside us. Psalms reminds us and gives us permission to lay out our questions, doubts, fears, rage, unfiltered thoughts, praise, celebration, and joy to God. It's as if he knows that the way toward divine union in worship is through a willingness to be human.

In Psalm 139, for instance, we see the heart of a person who is a model of deeply formed interior examination: David. The passage begins with him declaring,

O LORD, you have searched me and known me!
You know when I sit down and when I rise up;
　　you discern my thoughts from afar.
You search out my path and my lying down
　　and are acquainted with all my ways.
　　　　(verses 1–3)

The psalmist is overwhelmed not with grief but with gratitude and satisfaction because God knows him and claims him. God knows it all: the sadness and joy, the fears and lusts, the hopes and dreams. He sees the good in us, the bad in us, and the ugly in us. God knows us thoroughly.

The entire psalm is about David recognizing God's knowledge of him. In verses 7–8, David continued,

> Where shall I flee from your presence?
> If I ascend to heaven, you are there!
> If I make my bed in Sheol, you are there!

These words are not words of stalking or God using surveillance on us to catch us when we do wrong. David knows something about God. He knows that he is fully present to us. It's actually quite a beautiful image. Whether our thoughts are ascending toward God or we are floundering in the depths of our most hellish circumstances (*Sheol*), he is there, fully present.

Then David wrote,

> You formed my inward parts;
>> you knitted me together in my mother's
>> womb.
> I praise you, for I am fearfully and wonderfully
>> made.
> Wonderful are your works;
>> my soul knows it very well. (verses 13–14)

David gave voice to the creative love of God, who forms and shapes us into a masterpiece of creations. We are fearfully and wonderfully made. The entire psalm up until this point is about God's knowledge of humanity and David in particular.

But by the end of the passage, you get this sense that David was keenly aware that although God knew everything about him, David didn't know everything about himself. So in words of interiority and confession, he wrote,

> Search me, O God, and know my heart!
>   Try me and know my thoughts!
> And see if there be any grievous way in me,
>   and lead me in the way everlasting!
>   (verses 23–24)

Lord, show me *me*.

Oftentimes our prayers are, *Lord, show us* your *glory.* It's the great prayer of Moses in Exodus 33:18. But to complement that prayer, we need David to show us the way. We also need to be praying, *Lord, show me* me. Most of us want an awareness of God. But what we need in addition is awareness of self. David affirmed that God knows it all, so he asked for revelation not of God but of himself. The disposition of David's heart was to go beneath the surface.

Throughout this book thus far, I have highlighted the importance of listening. The contemplative way is about listening deeply to God. The way of reconciliation entails listening deeply to each other. The way of interior examination is about deeply listening to ourselves. In order to do this, we need a theology of examination for the purpose of self-awareness.

A SHORT THEOLOGY OF INTERIOR EXAMINATION

For centuries, people have extolled the virtue of self-examination. Socrates said, "The unexamined life is not worth living." Saint Augustine wrote, "O God, let me know myself; let me know you." Ice Cube said, "You better check yo self before you wreck yo self."[3] Like I said: for centuries.

One of the most important theological statements of self-awareness and examination comes from Reformed theologian John Calvin. He wrote, "The knowledge of God and that of ourselves are connected. Without knowledge of self, there is no knowledge of God. Without knowledge of God, there is no knowledge of self."[4] The knowledge of self he speaks of is not identical with twenty-first-century psychotherapeutic sensibilities. Calvin has in mind a knowledge of our creatureliness—of our condition of sin. When we know we are caught in sin, the knowledge of God and our need for salvation clarify the connection.

I would add, however, that sin is not limited to morality and salvation as it's typically understood. Sin is a principle of captivity to a power that permeates and contaminates our human reality. *Sin* is the word Christians use to name not simply our failed acts but also our inner and outer captivity. If we embrace a fuller understanding of the nature of sin, knowledge of self extends beyond our obvious acts of transgression or our insufficiency to save ourselves. It also extends to the limits and failure of living lives marked by wholeness. God in Christ takes on our sin that we may live forgiven, free, and whole. This wholeness extends to every aspect of life.

Beyond this, there are many helpful biblical statements that speak of the urgent call to self-examination. I'll highlight four places in particular where this shows up in Scripture:

1. *Examination before coming to the Lord's Table.* "Let a person examine himself, then, and so eat of the bread and drink of the cup" (1 Corinthians 11:28). In this passage, Paul is highlighting the urgency of self-examination when coming to the table of communion. He alarmingly notes that Christians have been coming without taking the time to reflect on their ways. There's a fundamental split between the sacredness of the table and the flippancy by which they approach it. Paul warns that God's judgment has come to this congregation because of their lack of examination. It's a sobering portion of Scripture.

2. *Examination of faith.* "Examine yourselves, to see whether you are in the faith. Test yourselves. Or do you not realize this about yourselves, that Jesus Christ is in you?—unless indeed you fail to meet the test!" (2 Corinthians 13:5). Here Paul urges the church to pay careful attention to their lives and determine whether they are living consistently with the truth of God's abiding presence. This call for examination requires thoughtful reflection on our outer deeds and inner life.

3. *Examination of our ways.* Lamentations 3:40 says, "Let us test and examine our ways, and return to the LORD!" This verse arises out of a particular moment of judgment and exile. Jeremiah laments that the people of God have lived mindlessly, caught up in their own ways. He calls all of us who are God's people back to a careful examination of our ways.

4. *Examination of our work.* In Galatians 6:3–5, Paul explains, "If anyone thinks he is something, when he is nothing, he deceives himself. But let each one test his own work, and then his reason to boast will be in himself alone and not in his neighbor. For each will have to bear his own load."

This brief biblical treatment of self-examination provides a big-picture perspective of the kind of work spiritual formation entails. If we are to be faithful to God and live deeply formed lives, the work of self-examination is imperative.

Even so, many people still find it difficult to live this out. Maybe you're reading this and feeling uneasy about the prospect of this kind of work. You're not alone. Some find it challenging because they believe that looking within leads to self-absorption. While it is true that, if not careful, we can spend an inordinate amount of time looking within (which could lead to a preoccupation with every interior feeling), the goal of self-examination is not navel-gazing. The goal of self-examination is freedom—freedom from destructive thought patterns, inner messages, and the ways we wrongly perceive things.

Others refuse to go in this way because looking within might lead to despair. In the same way that we don't want to go to the doctor to examine strange lumps on our bodies, some people are too emotionally distressed to investigate their interior lives. What might we discover? Will the news be too much to handle? Although the fear is certainly a reality, despair doesn't have to be. Our faith is one marked by the interplay of crucifixion and resurrection. What often seems like the end is just preparation for a new beginning.

Author Andreas Ebert remarked that many people are afraid of being swallowed up in themselves:

> Many avoid the path of self-knowledge because they are afraid of being swallowed up in their own abysses. But Christians have confidence that Christ has lived through all the abysses of human life and that he goes with us when we dare to engage in sincere confrontation with ourselves. Because God loves us unconditionally—along with our dark sides—we don't need to dodge ourselves. In the light of this love the pain of self-knowledge can be at the same time the beginning of our healing.[5]

When we consider Psalms and other biblical texts as models for interior examination, we begin to see the priority given toward accessing and integrating the world within. But it takes some work. David, in Psalm 139, did three things effectively that we are invited to follow. He made time for interior examination, he was integrated enough to surrender his inner world to God, and he had the courage to face himself. In short, his life was deep enough to confront busyness and compartmentalization—trouble spots for most of us.

We often don't look within simply because of our pace of life. The psalmist David took time to carefully lift his soul to God in the form of songwriting. He made time to navigate his inner world and offer penetrating words of self-awareness. There's no getting around it. A life with God for the sake of interiority requires time. Parker Palmer described this inner life as being found in silence—as a "solitary process of reflection that helps us reclaim the 'ground of our being' and root ourselves in something larger and truer than our own egos."[6]

At New Life, we regularly integrate emotionally healthy skills at various seminars, small groups, staff meetings, and Sunday gatherings to help our community look within. There are moments when we invite people to reflect on their hopes and dreams or fears and anxieties. We ask them to name their complaints and preferences in order to live more integrated, whole lives. But on a regular basis, some folks have a hard time naming their hopes, dreams, preferences, and fears. When I ask why they might be stuck, many say something to the effect of, "Life has been so full and busy that I haven't thought about it much."

Limited reflection usually leads to dangerous reaction.

This level of busyness has severe implications. Limited reflection usually leads to dangerous reaction. When there's no space to process our inner worlds, we find ourselves mindlessly and instinctually reacting to the world around us.

COMPARTMENTALIZATION

The compartmentalizing of our lives remains one of the most dangerous temptations for a follower of Jesus. Compartmentalization, in this context, refers to a kind of splitting of ourselves in which we offer some parts of our lives to God but deny the rest. The insidious practice of splitting refers to the subconscious habit of disconnecting aspects of ourselves.

Instead of integrating the aspects of our lives that often seem contradictory and unpleasant, we cut ourselves off from them, which in turn leads toward divided and inauthentic lives. In an attempt to present ourselves as whole, complete, and healthy people, we ignore and suppress various aspects of our lives instead of seeing them as pieces that need to be held together and integrated under God's loving gaze.

Like a child hiding a broken figurine from his mother for fear of judgment, we hide broken parts of ourselves from others (and more importantly, from ourselves) in an attempt to deliver us from judgment. But our refusal to embrace and integrate our parts is a recipe for greater personal, relational, and social pain. Hoping for peace and wholeness in the world while ignoring our own divided and contradictory parts ensures that we don't have peace in the world, in our families, and in our churches. David Benner, professor of psychology and spirituality, powerfully named this temptation we all have to deny particular "parts" of our lives. In his book *The Gift of Being Yourself,* he described the challenge:

> Genuinely transformational knowing of self always involves encountering and embracing previously unwelcomed parts of self. While we tend to think of ourselves as a single, unified self, what we call "I" is really a family of many part-selves. That in itself is not a particular problem. The problem lies in the fact that many of these part-selves are unknown to us. Even though they are usually known to others, we remain blissfully oblivious of their existence.[7]

This is the trouble we find ourselves in. It is impossible to experience wholeness while we regularly split off from our "part-selves." Benner named the value and possibility for healing when we invite our parts to connect to the larger frame of our lives.[8]

It is impossible to experience wholeness while we regularly split off from our "part-selves."

There is enormous value in naming and coming to know these excluded parts of self. My playful self, my cautious self, my exhibitionistic self, my pleasing self, my competitive self, and many other faces of myself—they all are parts of me, whether I acknowledge their presence or not. Christian spirituality involves acknowledging all our part-selves, exposing them to God's love, and letting him weave them into the new person he is making.

I'm reminded of a conversation I had with a nurse as I was preparing for my annual physical examination. It accomplished the exact opposite of what Benner described. The nurse began the preliminary steps of the examination with a series of questions, rapid-fire style. Somewhere in the course of the conversation before the exam, I told her I'm a pastor. She seemed quite pleased to be helping a clergyman. She arrived at the portion of questions that assessed my emotional health. She asked, "Do you have regular bouts with sadness or depression?"

I told her no.

At that moment, her Christian training skyrocketed to the surface as she enthusiastically said, "Amen. Depression is not of God."

Now, I understood exactly what she meant at that moment, but it was quite clear that she had a particular theology that made no room for the difficult part-selves that come with being human. However, the degree to which we are able to hold all of ourselves together is the degree to which we live with integrity, joy, and peace.

The act of holding all our parts together before God requires that we grow in awareness of ourselves. It's impossible to hold together what we don't even know exists. The deeply formed life cannot flourish without a commitment to interior examination. As Jesus cautioned, in the gaining of the world, we can easily lose our souls (see Mark 8:36). There is more to us than what we see, and the gospel gives us the courage to search and surrender all of our being to God.

SIX

Deeply Formed Practices of Interior Examination

The week of Thanksgiving 2018 was a particularly memorable one for me. It was the week that an important shift in my soul took place.

My wife, our two kids, and I had been preparing to head down from Queens to North Carolina to spend Thanksgiving at my cousin's home. The drive was roughly ten hours. My parents and sister, who live in Florida, were going to drive up ten hours. We would meet in the middle of our respective journeys and celebrate for a couple of days. We had planned this gathering for weeks. I was particularly excited about it, as we hadn't spent Thanksgiving with my parents in more than five years. My cousin and his wife prepared their home for the seven additional family members. It promised to be a wonderful few days . . . until I received a text from Rosie.

On Monday of that week, our daughter, Karis, was running a fever. She was not herself at all. Because we had a day before we were going to start our drive down, Rosie suggested that I take Karis to her pediatrician to ensure that the long drive wouldn't be too much for her. I scheduled the appointment immediately.

A couple of hours later, Karis was being examined by her doctor. I raised the issue of the drive down to North Carolina and received a positive response. I called Rosie immediately, joyfully letting her know of the good news. I could tell, however, that Rosie was still a bit uneasy, but she said she was okay with the decision to drive down the next day.

After Karis and I got home, I had to pick up a few items from the local supermarket. While getting back into the car to head home, I noticed that Rosie had sent me a text. As I read the text, I began to feel deep irritation, which led to anger and an overflowing sense of dismissiveness. Her text said, "I'm anxious about taking the trip to North Carolina with Karis not feeling well." I stared at the phone for a good forty-five seconds. I texted back that I'd be home in twenty minutes and we could discuss it more then.

For the next ten minutes, I was beside myself. I started talking out loud in the car. "We've planned this for weeks. Everyone made sacrifices. The doctor said it would be okay. If we were driving down to be with her parents, I bet she wouldn't think this." On and on, my assumptions, frustrations, and plans for convincing her flowed through my mind. But after those ten minutes, something shifted in me. My grip on the steering wheel loosened, my clenched jaw relaxed, and my breathing slowed.

You see, for the past three weeks, I had been paying close attention to how I reacted to the actions and words of others, especially those closest to me. On my drive home, I looked a bit deeper at my own interior world.

Thankfully, I had a few minutes for this kind of reflection before I returned home. Was I truly angry at Rosie because of her suggestion that we stay home? The answer became plain to see. The real issue in this situation was not my anger at Rosie but my anxiety at the prospect of having to call my parents and cousin. This was the undercurrent at work in me. I was afraid that they would be disappointed with me. I was concerned that they would see me in a different light. I was anxious that I would ruin the holiday for them. This whole situation was not about Rosie at all; it was about me.

I decided that I would walk into our home and take the time to listen to Rosie's concerns. By God's grace, I had already resolved that after talking with her, if she still wanted to stay home, I would be fine with this decision. I would immediately call my parents (who were already on their way) and let them know we couldn't make it. Would it have been a hard call to make? Absolutely. But I was determined not to have my actions ruled by my anxiety.

I got home and sat with Rosie, knee to knee, eye to eye. I asked her to tell me more about what she was feeling. In the past when I did this, I was already thinking about my response to her and the reason why her course of action was not the best. (Admittedly, this is something I still wrestle with.) She expressed her anxiety about Karis, as well as the mounting stress she felt about us moving to a new home the following week. We had a lot to pack, and there was still so much to do for that move. All of it greatly overwhelmed her.

Our conversation lasted about fifteen minutes. I listened intently and repeated back to her what I was hearing. I shared my own thoughts on the matter and the disappointment I would feel if we didn't go, but I did my best to share this with her in a noncoercive way. By the end of our talk, I told her that I had heard her and had no problem calling my family to tell them this new information. I truly meant it. After saying this, she thanked me for listening and concluded that she thought we could make the trip after all. Inside, I thought, *Thank God! That phone call would have been tough.* The trip turned out great.

I share this story not to position me as husband of the year but as a way of highlighting how rare this kind of listening was for me. (Rosie can testify.) It's easy to be a listening presence in moments of low anxiety. But in times of high anxiety, it's another story. What was I doing? Very simply, this is the work of interior examination.

From the onset of my Christian journey, I've been greatly blessed to have mentors who have patiently led me along the path of self-examination, whether of past hurts or of my current feelings of disorientation. I have been exposed to relationships and environments that prioritized self-awareness and examination. Even so, the interior iceberg goes deep, and it seems as if I'm constantly learning more about myself. The journey never ends.

How do we come to a place where we experience moments of breakthrough, healing, and wholeness? We put into practice self-examination. In this chapter, we'll look at four areas where thoughtful self-reflection is vital if we ever hope to change. These practices provide access to the inner worlds we often have trouble navigating and contribute powerfully to the larger "root system" of deeply formed lives, enabling us to more effectively traverse the world of contemplative life, reconciliation, sexuality, and mission. A good place to begin when thinking about self-examination is with our families.

EXAMINING OUR FAMILY OF ORIGIN

It makes sense that a good place to begin self-examination is with our family of origin because it is the environment that has formatively shaped us. The developmental years of infancy, childhood, and adolescence have lasting effects on how we understand ourselves, others, and the world at large. The emotional attachment (or lack thereof) we experienced with our parents or caregivers sets us on particular trajectories.

When examining how we've been formed by our families, it's helpful to keep in mind three categories: patterns, trauma, and scripts.

When examining how we've been formed by our families, it's helpful to keep in mind three categories: patterns, trauma, and scripts. All three categories—when we are not aware of them—coalesce to negatively form us in deep ways.

Patterns

Patterns are the repeated behaviors, practices, habits, or ways of thinking that extend from one generation to the next. The importance of naming patterns is that it situates us in reality. The battles we all face are not new. They often have been the battles of our parents, grandparents, and great-grandparents. As we like to say at New Life, "Jesus might live in your heart, but Grandpa lives in your bones." By this we mean that all of us have inherited positive legacies as well as negative ones. Whether the legacies are related to the healthy management of money, the love of art, or a commitment to joyful recreation, most of us can name a few positive legacies we've received.

On the other hand, we have our share of negative legacies that also get repeated. Whether these legacies are related to workaholism, conflict avoidance, or an inability to have committed relationships, patterns get repeated. What can further complicate these patterns is the reality of our surroundings, including our ethnic cultures, the larger cultural moment we live in, and our religious environments. But for now let's limit our focus to our families of origin.

It's remarkable to see the lights go on in someone's head upon realizing that his or her current experience looks eerily similar to that of previous generations. Moreover, it's often painfully fascinating to see patterns repeated by people who have actively wanted to put an end to a particular pattern. I've seen examples of men who hated their fathers and the alcoholism that defined them, only to find their lives under a similar power of addictive behavior. As we note the patterns from one generation to the next, we position ourselves for a shift in our self-understanding.

Trauma

When most people think of trauma, they think exclusively of catastrophic moments. But that is not the only way trauma works. Its presence often goes undetected, expressing itself in emotional distress that we consider to be normal. But make no mistake about it; to some degree or another, we carry experiences of trauma deep within.

When I talk about trauma, I have in mind two sides of the same coin: getting what I didn't deserve, and not getting what I did deserve. In the first case, many people experience abuse (physical, sexual, or emotional) or undergo dreadful periods of loss. These are painful, psychologically scarring moments that can last a lifetime.

In the second case, trauma is experienced due to what child psychiatrist Donald Winnicott refers to as "nothing happening when something might profitably have happened."[1] In some homes, even though our parents or caregivers were always around, we never received the nurture, warmth, or attachment that we needed in order to flourish. Many families didn't know how to create environments in which we felt safe and seen. I find this to be a normal human experience. Each family has gaps, and sometimes those gaps unfortunately result in insidious ripple effects. When examining our families of origin, taking inventory of our trauma provides space for the Spirit to bring about healing.

Additionally, trauma can be related to other experiences not directly a result of interpersonal pain. For example, when I was a child, my father used to hang out with his friends till the early hours of the morning. Every night he was out, I would hear gunshots from outside my window. Each night I heard shots, I would squeeze my eyes shut and curl up into a ball, thinking my father had been shot. To this day, whenever I hear the sound of gunshots, my body tightens and I'm somehow transported back in time. There is some underlying trauma at work, related to violence and a lack of security.

It's also important to note that just because a person didn't grow up with obvious dysfunction doesn't mean there's no underlying trauma. From time to time, I lead seminars in which I take people through their family-of-origin histories, and in the course of this exploration, some will say that they grew up in homes in which everything was fine. Certainly, there are some homes where parents are emotionally present, affirming, and bonding well with their children. But even in this environment, there might be gaps that remain. For some, the dysfunction was so normalized that they are incapable of seeing it.

Regardless of the homes you and I grew up in, paying attention to the emotional system of our families is critical for our well-being and wholeness. Psychoanalyst and philosopher Robert Stolorow explained that developmental trauma occurs when "emotional pain cannot find a relational home in which it can be held."[2] In other words, the pain we experience through everyday life has a way of metastasizing, damaging the rest of our emotional worlds.

As we uncover the ways we've been formed by our families, the goal is not simply to name what happened and the persons responsible. Although that certainly can get us out of illusion, the goal is to relate to our present pain in ways that reframe how we've internalized our experiences. In short, one of the major tasks of family-of-origin examination is the naming and rejection of certain scripts in favor of life-giving messages.

Scripts

Scripts are the messages we receive, the roles we are given, and the ways we believe we must live that have been consciously handed to us or subconsciously interpreted by us. Scripts can be related to a particular big moment in our history or the steady accumulation of little moments. When examining our family-of-origin formations, the naming of scripts provides interior revelation and positions us for the new scripts of the gospel. Let me share how this has worked out in my life.

I had an experience as an eleven-year-old that marked me deeply. It was related to my parents. Thankfully, my parents have been married more than forty years, and they would attest that the latter years have been better than the former. The former years were often very turbulent.

One weekday morning, I overheard my parents in an argument. At the time, my parents had just entered their thirties. They were still figuring out married life. I'm not sure of the reason, but my father didn't want to go to work that morning. He was tired. My mother, who rarely missed a day of work and carried a lot of financial anxiety, was incredibly agitated, as this was not the first time they'd had this conversation.

In the room adjacent to my parents' bedroom, while lying in bed, I overheard some of this conversation and thought that if dad was staying home from work, I wanted to stay home from school to be with him. When my mother walked over to my room to get me up for school, I told her I wanted to stay home too. At that moment, she lost it.

She had some choice words for me and then walked back over to my father and shouted some choice words at him. He ignored her, staying under the blanket. In her exasperated anger, she threw a pillow at him. Upon getting hit, he sprang to his feet with surprising energy that betrayed his tiredness, took the same pillow, and threw it back at her. She got up close to his face and shoved him. He shoved her back onto the bed, where she landed on my six-month-old sister, Melissa. I'd been watching this from a distance, and when I saw my sister crying, I ran into the room. I picked her up, stood between my parents, weeping and begging them to stop.

In that moment, something shifted in me. No script was consciously handed to me, but the internalized message of *I have to hold everything together* was lodged in my heart and mind. This script has marked my life. It has informed my decisions at home, my leadership at church, and my self-understanding. I have often lived with a sense of being overly responsible, afraid of failure, and excessively anxious in conflict, with the persistent feeling that I had to be a stable, unanxious person. No wonder I became a pastor. I have often given the impression that everything was going fine and have struggled to maintain limits.

The work of examining my family-of-origin scripts has given me a window into my soul and an opportunity to believe and orient my life around the good news of the gospel. The gospel says, "[Jesus] is before all things, and in him all things hold together" (Colossians 1:17). Whenever the scripts of my family of origin surface, my soul needs to return to this truth. But unless I'm doing the work of examination, I will not locate the source of the wounded ways I've been formed.

The goal of the genogram is to move to-ward greater healing for the purpose of loving well.

The three family-of-origin influences (patterns, trauma, and scripts) serve as a cocktail of de-formation, entrench-ing us in ways of thinking and behaving that require pa-tient and honest self-examination. To this end, one of the best tools for examining our family-of-origin formations and to help us quickly name areas that need to be healed is the genogram. The genogram is a family systems theory resource to help people visually see the patterns, trauma, and scripts that have formed their place in the world. At New Life, we lead people at various points in the year to examine their families of origin through the genogram.

The goal of the genogram is not simply to see the dys-function of our families (and it's definitely not to pro-voke us to hate our families). The goal of the genogram is to move toward greater healing for the purpose of lov-ing well.[3]

EXAMINATION OF OUR ANXIETY

The interior examination of anxiety is another powerful practice to engage in. To be anxious is to be human. But to be regularly shaped by anxiety diminishes our humanity. Therapist and pastor Peter Steinke noted two types of anxiety: acute and chronic.[4] Acute anxiety is situational and time based. It is a momentary loss of self-composure and poise. Chronic anxiety is not specific to a threat. Any issue, topic, or circumstance can provoke chronically anxious people. Consequently, they have little capacity to step out of their experience, observe their own emotionality, reflect on what is happening, make choices based on principles, and manage their lives.

It's normal to have moments of acute anxiety, but when our lives are chronically being affected by an undercurrent of anxious forces, we are in bondage. However, anxiety—although unpleasant—can provide us with the gift of self-awareness and healing. As we name our anxiety and its corresponding stories, we give ourselves the opportunity to rise above it.

Time and time again, God invites his people to come out from debilitating fear and into a deeper experience of peace and trust. When we examine our anxiety, we can expose the power and grip it has on our lives in place of God's great love.

I have found a helpful question to consider when identifying and examining anxiety: Who and what situations make me anxious? In my case, one of the people who has made me anxious (over the past ten years) has been the chairperson of our church board of elders. In my tenure as a lead pastor, we have had three different people in this role, and in each case—no matter who is in this role—I'm aware of my anxiety. There have been times when difficult conversations have been necessary; whenever something I've said or done needs clarification or leads to some critique, my anxiety surfaces. I've learned that I have a strong need to feel competent and capable, so anytime I infer that someone perceives me as not having these traits, my sense of self is wounded.

In the last few years, the gospel truth of grace has helped me be "compassionately curious" with myself whenever anxiety surfaces. I remember going through my annual performance review with the board of elders some years ago. During and after the meeting, I fixated on the minor points of correction they asked me to consider. It took days for me to shake my feelings of incompetence.

But the following year, something changed. I was learning to be compassionately curious. The board still had recommendations for how I could lead more effectively, and I noticed my anxiety rising. But this time, instead of going down a road of anxious self-loathing, I spent time asking myself why their comments affected me so much. When I returned home, I took twenty minutes to write down what I sensed was happening on the inside and then reminded myself that, like every other person on the planet, I have gaps and blind spots. And I will always have shortcomings and failings, as I'm a fallible human being.

When I have done a simple exercise like this, the lingering effects of my anxiety are limited. In the past, it might have taken a few days to move through some of the anxious moments I've experienced. As I have done this work, within a matter of hours, sometimes minutes, I have found myself being self-regulated.

EXAMINATION OF OUR FEELINGS

The examination of our feelings as a whole is an integral practice for deeply formed lives. To that end, I have found Alice Miller's distinction between emotions and feelings to be enlightening. She wrote, "Emotion is a more or less unconscious, but at the same time vitally important physical response to internal or external events—such things as fear of thunderstorms, rage at having been deceived, or the pleasure that results from a present we really desire. By contrast, the word 'feeling' designates a *conscious* perception of an emotion."[5]

The processing of our feelings leads us to live more integrated in the world, yet it's a path many people find difficult. Many of us have grown up with rules about feelings. In some cultures, to show any sign of sadness is to communicate weakness. In others, to express anger is frowned upon. In some churches, any show of grief is a sign that one lacks faith. Consequently, many people learn to avoid, repress, or rationalize away difficult feelings. But we need our feelings to help us navigate our world as well as to discern God's will.

The theologian who has helped me the most in seeing our feelings as part of a deeply formed life is Ignatius of Loyola (1491–1556). After a tragic accident in which his knee was shattered in battle, Ignatius had extended periods for reflection and examination. In the course of his reading, praying, and conversations with multiple people, he discovered the role of feelings in locating ourselves in the world and discerning God's will. In his classic work *The Spiritual Exercises,* Ignatius calls upon the religious faithful to a practice of examination. This involves bringing to mind the presence of God in an ordinary day, noting the ways in which we have been present to or unaware of God's presence. But one of the ingenious elements of Ignatian spirituality is the commitment to exploring the landscape of feelings. Ignatius called them consolations and desolations.

Consolations and desolations reveal feelings of peace, joy, and contentment, as well as feelings of angst, anger, and discontentment. But more than just naming the feelings, the goal is to lift the various feelings to help us discern if we are moving toward God or away from him. There are many layers to this approach, but for our purposes, the presence and processing of our feelings is to help us examine ourselves in light of God's presence. As we sift through these feelings, we not only provide outlets for potentially soul-damaging effects but also have another means of communing with God and others. Emotions don't die; they get redirected in a myriad of dangerous ways.

Toward this end, Pete and Geri Scazzero created a straightforward, powerful tool called Explore the Iceberg.[6] The tool offers four simple questions that the most intelligent and educated have struggled to respond to. It's a helpful guide for cultivating a life of interior examination. The four questions are:

1. What are you mad about?

2. What are you sad about?

3. What are you anxious about?

4. What are you glad about?

As we wrestle with these questions, whether in solitude or in community, we bring to light some of the material that needs to be named, discerned, and healed.

EXAMINATION OF OUR REACTIONS

Our reactions are a source of important revelation for our lives. They tell us more about ourselves than about other people. I mentioned earlier that in the Thanksgiving conversation with my wife, I had been paying attention to my reactions. There is a reason for that. I don't know about you, but there are times when my reactions to people, moments, news, or experiences are disproportionate to the actual event.

Our reactions are a source of important revelation for our lives.

There have been times when I notice an email from that person (we all have *that* person), and just seeing their name creates uneasiness in me. There are instances when I go down a road in my mind, envisioning how a situation might play out, and still it doesn't unfold how I anticipated. We all sometimes have disproportionate reactions to various encounters and experiences.

The key is asking questions that are introspective in nature, such as, *Why am I reacting this way? What is causing me to feel this angst?* and *Why am I so triggered by this person?* As we make sense of our reactions, we position ourselves to experience greater freedom. We will also find that our reactions can change, limiting the negative effects they might have on us. Let me give you an example from a conversation I had with a congregant.

After every Sunday worship service, I stand in the lobby of our building to connect with people from our congregation. On one recent occasion, a young woman approached me and asked if she could have a word with me. I stepped a couple of feet to the side to avoid the congregational traffic jam and listened intently.

She told me that something I had said in the sermon bothered her. I had been preaching about prayer and had shared a particular anecdote that she'd perceived as condescending and insensitive. After listening for a moment and asking a few clarifying questions, I attempted to explain what I meant. She didn't see it and reiterated her perception of that preaching moment. The conversation lasted a long four or five minutes, and we both walked away agreeing to disagree.

A few weeks later, I was greeting congregants again in the lobby. This time it was after the third and final service of the day. As I was in conversation with someone, I saw out of the corner of my eye that the same young woman was waiting for me. *Oh no, what did I say now?* I thought.

She waited patiently for me to finish greeting others and approached me. I think I greeted her a bit too enthusiastically to compensate for the tension I thought I would experience again, but she went right into the conversation. "Pastor Rich, do you recall the conversation we had a few weeks ago?"

"Yes, I do," I replied.

She then said, "Since that time, I've been thinking

about my reaction to your sermon. I've come to realize that I wasn't really bothered by your words. That wasn't the root problem. Your words inadvertently triggered a nagging feeling of shame that I've carried for years from my family of origin. I've started to address that area of brokenness in my life. I hope I didn't come across as disrespectful or condescending."

> In the examination of our reactions, we live from a place of depth, wisdom, and discernment.

My eyes opened with delight, relief, and conviction. I've certainly said my fair share of things that have genuinely offended people, but in this case, a mature, self-reflective congregant did the work of self-examination, revealing my own deficiencies in this area. I had not taken the time to do what she had done. It was a wonderful pastoral-growth moment, reminding me that our reactions hold key insights for our own transformation.

In the examination of our reactions, we live from a place of depth, wisdom, and discernment. We find ourselves in a better place to reject the lies and stories that often distort our vision. Our perceptions become clearer; we make fewer assumptions and live without the heavy burden of self-justification, self-condemnation, and the need to judge others.

In the fall of 2018, for a month's time I decided that I would take inventory of my reactions. I noticed that I was being easily triggered by criticisms and I carried a nagging sense of uneasiness about difficult conversations that needed to be had. I resolved that if I found myself negatively or disproportionately reacting to someone or something, I would take a few minutes during the day to process that moment through five questions:

1. *What happened?*

2. *What am I feeling?*

3. *What is the story I'm telling myself?*

4. *What does the gospel say?*

5. *What counter-instinctual action is needed?*

In the simplicity of wrestling with these questions, I became freer. For that month, I engaged in this practice almost daily. In so doing, I noticed how emotionally fragile and fearful I had been with certain people in particular. In the processing of these questions (sometimes for ten minutes, sometimes thirty or more), I began to see some of the lies I'd been believing. Let me give a short example.

One day I received an email from a well-known Christian leader and author. She is someone I respect and have learned from. She noticed a resource for prayer that I had posted on social media and in a thoughtful, kind way asked if I would consider making some adjustments on the resource so a larger community of people could benefit from it.

For some reason, her email message triggered me. Although there was not a single unkind word in the message, upon reading it the first and second time, I perceived the email as a slight. I thought, *Who does she think she is sending me this?* I found myself somewhat embarrassed that I had not anticipated the change she suggested and closed my laptop in an effort to move away from that moment. About fifteen minutes later, I decided to examine my reaction. This is my (shortened) journal entry:

- *What happened?* A well-known leader offered constructive feedback.

- *What am I feeling?* Shame.

- *What is the story I'm telling myself?* If I don't do things right the first time (or ever, for that matter), I'm defective.

- *What does the gospel say?* My failures and mistakes don't define me; God's love does.

- *What counter-instinctual action is needed?* Share this story with Rosie (which was counter-instinctual for me because I tend to keep moments like this to myself).

Sometime during that month's practice, I noticed my triggers starting to diminish. I found myself less bothered by criticism and feedback. I was able to see many of the reactions for what they were: moments for healing brought forth by the gospel. Do I still get triggered? Absolutely. Do I still need healing from destructive scripts? Indeed. But something had shifted in my soul.

The number of times I've had to sit and process my emotions in this way has subsided. There's the ongoing work of formation that I still must engage in, but my journey of capturing and examining my reactions has set me on a path toward a greater sense of freedom.

The goals of self-examination are threefold. First, through these practices, we open ourselves up to the grace and presence of God. The truth is, we are all in the same boat of needing a regular rhythm to help us to grow in awareness of our blind spots, shadow sides, and hidden sins.

Second, we live in the world with greater freedom, untangling ourselves from the web of inner dysfunction and confusion. The practice of looking within is not to be an act of masochism but a choice to honor our own feelings without shame or judgment.

Third, we become a presence in this world, more capable of working toward peace with our neighbors and love for those who might be considered enemies. In the Sermon on the Mount, Jesus instructed us to take the way of self-examination, removing the logs from our own eyes that we may see the specks of dust in our neighbors' eyes (see Matthew 7:5; Luke 6:42). The world is in desperate need of people willing to examine their own selves before examining others. The work of "other-examination" comes all too naturally. We are accustomed to viewing, judging, and comparing others rather than ourselves. That's easy. The way of self-examination is hard. But by God's grace, the Spirit can help us.

SEVEN

Sexual Wholeness for a Culture That Splits Bodies from Souls

In 2016, following the death of the pop icon Prince, the *New York Times* published an article titled "Prince's Holy Lust." The writer suggested there are two keys to understanding the man and his music: his sexuality and his spirituality. The article went on to say that for Prince, a Jehovah's Witness, "the love of God and the sexual urges we feel are one and the same somehow. For him it all comes from the same root inside a human being. God planted these urges and it's never wrong to feel that way. The urge itself is a holy urge."[1]

We might look at Prince's life and rightfully conclude that his understanding of sexuality and spirituality didn't reflect the sexual ethic of Jesus and the kingdom of God. But one thing that we can all learn from Prince is the importance of integrating these two powerful realities of life. Prince, albeit imperfectly, explored the relationship between these two themes in his songs, and we, too, need to pay attention to the relationship between sexuality and spirituality if we are to navigate this life well. On this point, Prince had incredible insight: our sexuality and spirituality are connected.

We struggle to live with a mature, deeply human and humane, anxiety-free vision of our bodies as it relates to our spirituality.

Sadly, over the course of history, the church has not succeeded much at making this connection. Consequently, so many of us are ill equipped to engage in any meaningful conversation along these lines. We struggle to live with a mature, deeply human and humane, anxiety-free vision of our bodies as it relates to our spirituality.

Ron Rolheiser noted that throughout history, there has been a "divorce in Western culture between religion and eros. Like all divorces it was painful, and as in all divorces, the property got divided up: Religion got to keep God and the secular got to keep sex. The secular got passion and the God got chastity."[2] It's important to point out that in his usage of the word *chastity*, Rolheiser was critiquing popular notions of how chastity is understood, not diminishing it as a powerful and sacred way of life. But his point is well taken. The question remains, How do we "remarry" religion and *eros*? Or said another way, How do we join spirituality and sexuality in ways that lead to greater wholeness in our relationship with God and with others? This is what I'd like to explore in this chapter and the next.

My intention is not to wade into the important and multifaceted layers of sexuality that include sexual orientation, transgenderism, and the social and political tensions that exist inside and outside the church. There are many other helpful resources along those lines. My goal is to provide a pathway that helps us make sense of our emotional and sexual longings and to show how our bodies have everything to do with God and our spiritual development.

WHAT IS SEXUALITY?

At the core of this relationship between sexuality and spirituality is desire and longing. What we do with our sexual desires and longings says a lot about what we believe about God. This is why we need to clearly define terms.

Defining *spirituality* and *sexuality* can seem like a daunting task because there is much confusion surrounding these words. To offer a simpler way forward, I have found speaker and author Debra Hirsch's definitions instructive:

> *Spirituality* can be described as a vast longing that drives us beyond ourselves in an attempt to connect with, to probe and to understand our world. And beyond that, it is the inner compulsion to connect with the Eternal Other, which is God. Essentially, it is *a longing to know and be known by God (on physical, emotional, psychological and spiritual levels)*. . . .
>
> *Sexuality* can be described as the deep desire and longing that drives us beyond ourselves in

an attempt to connect with, to understand,
that which is other than ourselves. Essentially,
it is *a longing to know and be known by other
people (on physical, emotional, psychological and
spiritual levels).*[3]

Along these lines, theologian Marva Dawn has per-
ceptively delineated two kinds of sexuality that often get
confused in our culture. Dawn noted that in Genesis 1
and 2, we are presented with two visions of sexuality:
social sexuality and genital sexuality. In Genesis 1, human
beings are created in the image of God and given the
holy task of relating to the rest of creation in ways that
declare the harmony and interdependence of all things.
As Dawn wrote, "Human beings are especially created to
image God, and a significant part of that imaging is fellowship. In our relationships with each other, we model
the community of the Trinity."[4] This longing for fellowship and belonging is stamped into the fabric of our
souls.

We long to be seen and to see others from the earliest
moments of human development. Whether in our living
rooms or on the playground, we long for connection—
for an immediate felt experience of closeness to another.
This is fundamentally what it means to be human. For
example, not too long ago I took my five-year-old son,
Nathan, to the playground. He found another little boy
to play with, and they chased each other all around the
park. The next morning, Nathan asked if we could go to
the park again. I said yes, to which he responded, "Daddy,
I need to wear the same shirt I wore yesterday."

"Why, son?" I asked. He responded, "Because my friend

won't remember me if I have a different shirt on." It was a really cute moment. But beyond the cuteness, his desire to belong and be seen was on display. This is social sexuality: the longing we all have to deeply bond with others and to be seen and known, to know and to see.

In Genesis 2:24, however, we see another dimension of sexuality. God lovingly established a means of covenant love whereby man "is commanded to leave his father and mother and cleave to his wife."[5] Dawn explained that this new family unit is "especially marked by the covenantal sign of genital union."[6] In this portion of Scripture, the belonging takes on a particular form. Through the act of sexual union, we express with our entire bodies the call to full-covenant love and union. In this powerful and creative act, we vulnerably offer ourselves to another, mysteriously reflecting the interpenetrative love of the Trinity. Genital sexuality is not just about our bodies colliding with each other; it's an act of self-giving, mutually indwelling love that points to something beyond ourselves. That is why this kind of love requires the powerful and nurturing safeguard found in marriage.

To have our lives deeply formed toward sexual wholeness, we must discern and distinguish these two kinds of sexuality. Otherwise, we aim our desires in directions that aren't meant to meet the longings of our souls. For example, many in our culture have assumed that the desire to truly belong and be seen by another requires an act of genital sexuality. In the process, we dangerously open ourselves up to others in the most vulnerable way (nakedness) to meet a need that doesn't require us to take off our clothes. As Dawn wrote, "I am convinced that, if the Church could provide more thorough affection and care for persons, many would be less likely to turn falsely to genital sexual expression for the social support they need."[7]

Dawn's words ring true. It's true of all of us that at some point in our lives, we have looked for love in all the wrong places. Consequently, we live with the profound sense of our sexual brokenness. This is the story of humanity from the opening pages of Scripture.

SIN, SHAME, AND OUR BODIES

From the very beginning, the human story has been one of deep conflict and alienation with our bodies. The first few pages of the Bible capture the glorious communion experienced by humanity with God and with each other and then dramatically shifts to the tragic estrangement that has characterized the human family ever since.

Genesis 1 and 2 begin with God's good creation. The Bible is off to a wonderful start. God creates a beautiful world marked by abundance, beauty, diversity, and delight. God lovingly and generously shares this world with humanity, creating Adam and Eve to be stewards of the created order. So far, so good.

The author of Genesis continues to elaborate on the wholeness, purity, and freedom experienced in the garden between the man and the woman. In one of the most scintillating verses in all the Bible, it reads, "The man and his wife were both naked and were not ashamed" (2:25). Here we have humanity living in the greatest of joy and freedom. Their love for each other is free from body shaming, free from comparison, free from objectification. There is a fundamental unity between their God, their surrounding creation, and their bodies.

As the story goes, God gives them a tour of a fully furnished paradise and sets an important boundary in place: they aren't supposed to eat from the tree of the knowledge of good and evil. In creating this boundary, God is establishing the dignity and capacity for freedom within humanity. He creates the conditions for choice— being able to volitionally love, free of coercion—which is essential for souls created in his likeness. Soon after, a serpent comes on the scene, seducing them into eating from the tree. Now we read one of the most tragic verses in the Bible: "The eyes of both were opened, and they knew that they were naked. And they sewed fig leaves together and made themselves loincloths" (3:7).

Prior to this "fall," Adam and Eve didn't live blind to each other's bodies; they saw each other. Yet their gazes didn't begin and end with a fixation of each other's body parts but rather in the wholeness of their being. Their bodies were certainly objects of desire, but not in such a way that their desire objectified the other. They saw the contours and curves of each other, but they also saw the larger construction of their humanity. They looked upon each other with sacred and sensual eyes, communing joyfully with each other. They were exposed but not ashamed, vulnerable but not self-conscious, laid bare without the need for self-protection.

But upon their disobedience, sin distorts their vision, ironically, by opening their eyes. Prior to this moment, they saw with the pure eyes of God. Now they see with the marred vision of human fallenness. Their eyes being opened is the anti-miracle of the New Testament. In the New Testament, Jesus repeatedly opened blind eyes, helping people see physically as well as spiritually. But in this Genesis 3, the way sin opens humanity's eyes paradoxically cuts off the deeper vision by which we are to see each other. We now live ashamed by our exposure, self-conscious of our vulnerability, and needing to protect ourselves from being laid bare.

To sum it up, our sexuality is perverted by a powerful root of shame.

More than just feeling guilt or existential dread, Adam and Eve find themselves in shameful estrangement with their bodies because of their estranged relationship with God. They hide from each other and from God. From this point on, the human experience is marked more by using than by communion, more by a destructive separation of body and soul than by a body-soul unity, more by a paralyzing preoccupation with our bodies rather than a holy unawareness.

To sum it up, our sexuality is perverted by a powerful root of shame. Locating shame in our lives is actually quite a simple exercise. If we took a moment to identify areas we have great difficulty naming, shame is usually the reason for our propensity to hide and conceal.

Thankfully, the story doesn't end with ultimate judgment. However, lasting and terrible consequences follow and will continue to haunt humanity. God finds Adam and Eve and offers them a word of hope, but by this time, the damage is done. They are under a different kind of power now. Humanity is not bereft of an ability to love well, but our desires are disordered.

THE THREE DIETS OF SEXUAL FORMATION

To further name this disorder of our desires, I have found author and speaker Christopher West's categories of sexual formation insightful. In his book *Fill These Hearts,* he presented three "diets" that speak to the ways the church and the surrounding world understand sexuality and spirituality: the starvation diet, the fast-food diet, and the banquet.[8] In other words, we have often had our understanding of sexuality formed by sexual repression or sexual flippancy, and in the process we have missed the larger feast before us. These diets are frameworks to help us better grasp the disintegration we experience as well as the integration of our humanity available in the gospel.

Starvation Diet

Many people of faith live on a starvation diet. It's the diet that sees our longings and desires (particularly our sexual longings and desires) as aspects of our humanity that need to be rejected, suppressed, or ignored. This kind of theology permeates our churches so much that even talking about desire, sex, longings, and eros is done in whispers. Sex and sexuality are territories to be avoided at all costs. Instead of the church being the community and place to help people make sense of their longings, the longings are seen as antithetical to a robust spirituality. A small sampling of movements and prominent figures throughout church history show this to be an ongoing disorder.

In the third century, Origen (an influential father of the church) viewed sexual passion as an obstacle to experiencing true joy in God. According to him, "Physical pleasure and sexual experiences nurtured a counter sensibility. They resulted in a dulling of the spirit's true capacity for joy."[9] Origen believed that even in marriage, sexual intercourse "coarsened the spirit."[10] According to church tradition, he allegedly took his theology to its logical conclusion: he castrated himself so as to eliminate any desire for the women he would teach. Whether that is historically accurate or not, it is part of the pervasive narrative that informs how many people view the human experience; that is, sexual desire is bad and needs to be, well . . . cut off.

This starvation diet can also be seen in the writings of Saint Augustine, arguably the most influential theologian in church history. In his *Confessions,* Augustine articulated his struggle to maintain purity of life. As a young man, he was sexually active—a slave to his impulses. In one of his more amusing reflections, he prayed, "Give me chastity and self-restraint, but don't do it just yet."[11] In his striking conversion, he sought to love Christ with his body but found it extremely difficult to do so. Out of this struggle, he came to some theological conclusions that viewed sexual desire in pejorative ways. He classified his longings as obstacles that shut him out from loving union with God, as opposed to the energy within that points to union. Instead of aiming desire to its source in God, it was to be avoided at all costs.

This line of thinking would resurface throughout

church history in Revivalist, Holiness, Pentecostal, and Evangelical Purity movements, to name a few. Notoriously, in order to emotionally survive, those who subscribed to this diet often ended up living secret, duplicitous lives, looking for illegitimate outlets to meet their legitimate longings. Women were regularly scapegoated, being depicted as temptresses and shamed when word got out that they were sexually active.

The unfortunate consequence in this is seeing our bodies, pleasure, and sexuality as impediments to true spirituality. This mindset, however, is shaped more by Gnosticism than by a biblical vision of creation. Gnosticism is an ancient teaching that regarded the material world (our bodies in particular) as prisons from which our spirits must be set free. In the process of attaining gnosis (special knowledge), people are supposed to be released from the constraints of their physicality and ascend to unity with the great Spirit. Throughout the centuries, the pernicious heresy of Gnosticism has reared its head, trying to convince us that our bodies, desires, and longings are not as important as our souls.

Now certainly, there must be appropriate space within our lives with God to say no to some of the desires and passions that arise in us. In the season of Lent, the church emphasizes ascetic practices such as fasting to ground us in the notion that we are not to be exclusively governed by our appetites but by God's way and will. So for a season, we'll go without some of the things that bring us delight, and in so doing we live from a different center. The problem we fall into with this diet, however, is that it was never meant to be the only mode of faith and prac-

tice. Far too many Christians have lived as if Lent were a
year-round season of the church. But it's not.

In fact, to fast when God calls us to feast is a violation
of the highest order. We see this in the Gospels. Repeatedly, Jesus told his disciples to enjoy the feast that was
before them, knowing that there would come a time
when fasting would be the appropriate response to life.
In the gospel of Matthew, while speaking of his presence
among his followers, Jesus said, "Can the wedding guests
mourn as long as the bridegroom is with them? The days
will come when the bridegroom is taken away from them,
and then they will fast" (9:15). In other words, don't
subject yourself to something Jesus didn't command.
Many of us need to heed these words because we have
erroneously believed that God is only pleased in the sup-
pression of our passions.

Fast-Food Diet

If the starvation diet is about *repression,* the fast-food diet
is about *reduction.* This diet is the attempt to reduce our
deepest longings to our physical desires. Whereas the first
diet shapes many in the church, this diet is broadly consumed by many in the surrounding world. This diet says,
"Whatever your desire, you deserve to have it met. Does
it feel right? Then go for it." The fast-food diet is about
the casual posture people have toward sex and sexuality.
It's the inability or refusal to see sex as a sacred fire that,
when not treated with care, leads to entire lives and communities being burned.

The fast-food diet places humanity at the center of
sexual desire. There is no discernment regarding our

bodies. Our souls are split from our bodies in a similar but different way from the starvation diet. In the starvation diet, the soul is exalted to the point of denying the body. In the fast-food diet, the body is exalted to the point of denying the soul and the soul-numbing pain we've experienced. The danger of this diet is that it is a cheap imitation of the banquet (the third diet). Although you might feel satisfaction for the moment, it makes you sick.

The other danger of the fast-food diet is the unrealistic expectation we assign to the fulfillment of sexual desire. Although we have legitimate needs to connect (as Hirsch noted earlier), the fast-food diet doesn't see the bigger picture. C. S. Lewis aptly explained this:

> Creatures are not born with desires unless satisfaction for those desires exists. A baby feels hunger: well, there is such a thing as food. A duckling wants to swim: well, there is such a thing as water. [Humans] feel sexual desire: well, there is such a thing as sex. If I find in myself a desire which no experience in this world can satisfy, the most probable explanation is that I was made for another world.[12]

The world we were made for is not somewhere beyond the stars. The world we were made for is the home of God's love. But in the fast-food diet, we try to suck out infinity from finite sources. Eventually, we find that we have placed too much weight on other people or on sexual experiences to satisfy the deep needs of our souls. Yet we go on trying.

When love and intimacy are replaced with the flippant swiping left or right on social networking sites like Tinder or with the use of pornography, we end up in a vicious cycle of want. Other people become objects for our gratification. We lose touch with our humanity. We ravenously search for new ways to stimulate ourselves. Consequently, we find ourselves imprisoned, endlessly searching for what can be found only in God. There's a popular quote (often attributed to G. K. Chesterton) that says, "The man who rings the bell at the brothel, unconsciously does so seeking God." In other words, at the moments when our desires become illicit and we find ourselves trapped by their power, even then there is something deeper at work.

The starvation diet has no imagination to see sexual desire as a means toward God. The fast-food diet relegates sexual desire to being its god. Both are missing the point.

Banquet

The gospel offers us a banquet. That's what we all yearn for: a feast that doesn't just fill our bellies with tasty things but nourishes our souls as well. After a while, diets exclusively consisting of McDonald's are going to kill us. And dieting on ice cubes will never satisfy us. There is an invitation—whether married or single—to a life of communion, joy, and delight.

With the banquet diet, we are reminded that from the very beginning, humanity was made for community and intimacy with each other. We have often misplaced our longings and reaped the consequences, yet the offer remains. The sexual desires we possess, when ordered rightly, bring us to union with God and communion with each other. The love of God doesn't remove our desires; it reorders them.

The banquet is the recognition that we were created for ecstasy but that this ecstasy is found only in God. He is the ultimate source of our lives, joy, and sexual desire. The starting point and the end point of our desires is God. This is the work of good theology and spiritual formation—believing that our bodies and sexuality were meant to point to something outside ourselves.

In Jesus, the banquet is embodied as well as offered. Jesus is the fullness of humanity and divinity. He shows us what God is like and what humanity is invited into. He is the model we are called to emulate, which is to say that Jesus's sexuality was not diminished or disordered or deficient. When some of us think of Jesus, we imagine that he didn't have any sexual energy in his body. For many reasons, we'd like to think of him as asexual. But if he indeed is fully human, he must be fully sexual as well.

To be sexual doesn't mean to be sexually active, nor does it mean that Jesus lusted after others. He is the sinless Son of God, who fully participated in the human experience. We tend to believe that unless one is having intercourse with another person, his or her sexuality is not fully manifested. But that is not true. Jesus lives the human experience to the full, connecting with others intimately, compassionately, and sacrificially. In his death and in the Eucharist, he offers his body as a gift.

Jesus enters into loving union with others throughout his life and in so doing communes with the Father. The inverse is also true: Jesus lives in loving union with the Father and in so doing communes with the world. This is the banquet. Although it is true that sexual intercourse, flowing from the sacred context of marital covenantal love, is a beautiful sign of God's love, it is not the only way to living one's sexuality to the fullest.

CHRISTIANITY AND OUR BODIES

The deeply formed life takes seriously the New Testament claim that God took on human flesh. In the Incarnation, we locate the real presence of God in Jesus. When Jesus walked down the street, one could have accurately said, "There goes God." This is the mystery beyond mysteries. Yet the Incarnation is not limited to locating God in the flesh through Jesus; it is the lens by which we are to relate to the world. In Jesus's incarnation, death, and bodily resurrection, God unequivocally sanctified creation. Because God touched the world (literally), all that is seen and unseen radiates divine presence. That is why our response to the coming of God in Jesus is to see our bodies and the created order with profound sacredness.

The other day, I was watching a basketball game on television. An NBA player gave the jersey he played in—soaked with his perspiration—to a kid in the stands. The kid, overwhelmed with joy, began to cry. Because it was touched and worn by a basketball star, the jersey took on a life of its own. It was a qualitatively different jersey than the ones you can buy in the store. I imagine that the kid probably tried it on and then framed it. Something that valuable mustn't get damaged.

This is the essence of Jesus taking on flesh. In the story of Jesus, the Creator took on creation—took on a human body and, in self-giving love, sweat drops of blood. He died for the world and rose again. Our bodies have the marks of God on them, which is why we are to treat them with tender care. For this same reason, we are to be good stewards of the environment. God's kingdom is not good news for our bodies alone but for the entire material world.

A SACRAMENTAL LIFE

When people think of the word *sacrament,* such images as baptism and the Lord's Supper come to mind. In many Christian traditions, sacrament is a particular means of grace that God grants us. In less theological language, it's the vehicle God uses to drive home his love and favor in our hearts. The elements that are used in Christian sacramental theology (bread, wine, oil, and water) remind us that God uses the ordinary stuff of daily life to communicate something of God's loving presence among us. There's nothing magical about these elements, but when taken by faith, the Spirit works in mysterious ways. The elements point to a larger reality that is beyond our physical sight.

I went to a retreat many years ago at a monastery near Boston. As other retreatants were entering the sanctuary, I noticed each of them dipping their fingers in the small basin of water and placing the sign of the cross on their foreheads. Coming from the Pentecostal and Evangelical traditions, I didn't know what this was about. Was this some empty ritual to spare us from God's judgment as we entered into worship?

When it was my turn to enter, I self-consciously placed

my fingers in the basin, not knowing how deep it was and going in a bit too far. I dared not turn around to see what the person behind me was doing. I placed the water on my forehead, and a singular drop slid down my face. It looked as if I were crying.

I participated in the service and met with one of the monks the next day. I asked him, "What are you doing when you place your fingers in that holy water and make the sign of the cross on your forehead?" His answer, in its simplicity, was beautiful. He said that when you perform this act, the water reminds you of your baptism, and your baptism reminds you that you belong to Jesus. I sat there taking in those words. I belong to Jesus.

To put it simply, we are not just to receive sacraments; we are to become them.

Through the use of ordinary water, mixed with a faith that now understood its significance, my heart was drawn into the mystery of God's saving love. But the significance is not just in this moment. Sacramental living is a way of spiritual formation that sees all of creation as the means by which we can encounter the living God. He stands outside creation and simultaneously meets us through it. This has profound implications for our lives. If God is present through elements of water, bread, oil, and wine, he most certainly is present through our bodies as well. We are fearfully and wonderfully made. Our bodies, in their glory and fragility, in their energy and weakness, are means by which God meets us.

To put it simply, we are not just to receive sacraments; we are to become them. Whether through our compassionate love for our neighbors, shared intimacy with friends, kindness toward our children, or through the making of love with our spouses, our entire lives point to something beyond ourselves.

In the next chapter, I will offer a handful of practices that can set us off on a journey toward more deeply formed lives in our bodies and sexuality. There are many layers of formation that have shaped us that require discernment, careful nuancing, and in some cases, rejection. Our bodies, though affected by the reality of sin, are gifts from God to cherish and nurture.

When we think about our bodies and sexuality, it's often done under a burden of shame, regret, grief, and anger. Many of us have been wounded by others—abused, shunned, and ignored by people we expected would protect and nurture us. We have allowed our disordered passions to send us down roads of sin, pain, and death. We have used others and been used. We have received debilitating messages and been traumatized by destructive acts. We are all sexually broken in some way.

But this is not the end of our stories. There is hope. In power and love, God can form us deeply in the way of Jesus. In him, our bondage is overcome. Our wounds don't have the last word. Christ is victorious. In the opening pages of the Bible, we see the tragic effects of sin. After eating from the tree God forbade, Adam and Eve hid behind a tree, naked and conquered by shame.

This has been the story of humanity throughout the

ages. But it need not end there. In Jesus, a new humanity is offered: one not shackled by the prison of sin and shame but liberated into the fullness of God's love. In that singular act involving that tree in the Garden of Eden, the world was sent into a dangerous tailspin of sin. But then Jesus came and, in an act of obedience, forever changed the trajectory of the world.

Yes, Adam and Eve hid behind a tree, naked and conquered by shame. But Jesus hung on a tree, naked, and conquered shame. This is the good news of the gospel. In Jesus, shame doesn't have the last word. Our desires no longer need to be disordered. We can live in the freedom that comes in his name.

EIGHT

Deeply Formed Practices of Sexual Wholeness

I was struck by the title on *ESPN The Magazine: The Body Issue* recently. In an attempt to highlight the unique expressions of bodies in sports, *ESPN* features the naked bodies of athletes, angling their bodies in such a way to conceal the body parts you can't show outright. Each issue highlights people who have experienced bodily trauma, have perfectly sculpted bodies, or have bodies that are larger than others. *The Body Issue* doesn't seem to be driven by eroticism but by appreciation for the various manifestations bodies exhibit. But what caught my attention was the phrase "Every Body Has a Story."

Every *body*, indeed, has a story—of pain, pleasure, frustration, abuse, nurture, regret, shame, and love. I would say that most of us experience *all* these stories in our bodies, which suggests that throughout the course of our lives, we will have to wrestle with the stories of our bodies and relate to them and the bodies of others in deeply formed ways.

If we are awake and engaged, we will find ourselves asking a set of very promising questions:

- How do we honor our bodies? How do we honor the bodies of others?

- How can we reject in our daily lives the scripts, lies, and disordered appetites that entrench us in deeply de-formed ways?

- How can we work toward wholeness, healing, integrity, and love in this area of our lives?

- How do we love God well with our bodies and with our sexuality?

These questions together help us live into the larger question: What are the deeply formed practices of sexuality that can help us reflect God's desire for our world?

The practices, much like the other values in this book, will borrow from the contemplative tradition, the commitment to interior examination, and the urgent vision to see our bodies and sexuality as aspects of mission in the world. First, let's begin with naming the messages we've received.

THE PRACTICE OF NAMING
SEXUALLY DE-FORMED MESSAGES

What usually stands in the way of sexual wholeness are the sexual scripts we've inherited from our families and surrounding culture. In the course of our childhood de-

velopment, we have consciously and subconsciously received messages that have sent us down the wrong road.
Whether the messages were given by parents, extended
family, friends, the church, or TV, the layers of our sexual
formation run incredibly deep. As a child, I was exposed
to pornography around the age of twelve. Before I understood how my own body worked, I was tragically exposed to other bodies at work. The images remain, and
so do the messages.

Before I understood how my own body
worked, I was tragically exposed to other
bodies at work.

It would take many years into adulthood before I
would be set free from sexually addictive behavior (more
on that to come), but the ongoing work of formation has
been the naming and rejection of messages I've received.
Beyond pornography, I would casually hear friends, caregivers, and other adults dismissively speak of women and
relationships in demeaning ways. In the words of the famous philosopher Martin Buber, from his book *I and
Thou*, I was formed to see women as "its" and not "thous."
Women were not seen beyond their body parts. Consequently, the messages that ran deep in me sounded like
this: there are some bodies that are worthy of love and
others that are not; any impulse I have must be satisfied;
sex and sexual performance define me; and sex is only a
physical act, not a means of loving communication.

The messages run deep in all of us. Some messages

were inappropriately passed down; others were anxiously avoided, which only left room for uninformed and dangerous conclusions. For example, I once met with a congregant who struggled with sexual addiction. After he confessed to this, I asked him about his formation as a child. I asked him to tell me his earliest memory of discussing matters of sexuality. He recalled the moment with ease.

He told me how his father, reeking of alcohol, came into his room to have "the talk." As the thirteen-year-old was playing video games, his father swept in unannounced, sat down, and with a brown bag in hand began to give a lecture. Through fumbling words, his father explained the birds and the bees. After an excruciating five minutes of anxious and incoherent talking, the boy's father said, "You got it?" Leaning back with eyebrows raised, he nodded. The next moment, his father took a *Playboy* magazine out of the brown bag and said, "You can have this. Just put it in between your mattress so your mother doesn't see it." From that moment on, the teenager was hooked. In those five minutes of incoherent speech, there were crystal-clear messages handed down to this thirteen-year-old: sexuality is inherently an awkward topic, secrecy and sexuality go hand in hand, and if women don't look like what's in the magazine, something is wrong with them.

The act of naming our histories of sexual formation doesn't fully address the gaps and errors that shape our lives, but it can help us become aware of the lies and scripts that God invites us to lay down. For those who have been abused, this is a difficult undertaking. The trauma stored in our bodies is not undone simply by recalling our histories of formation. However, it is a start.

When we can expose the lies we've believed, we are in a position to welcome God's presence and power into our lives. God doesn't dwell in unreality and illusion. By naming the illusions and lies we've been handed, we open ourselves to the liberating truth of God's saving love.

A conscious practice like this gives us access to new sexuality scripts shaped by the gospel. You might believe that you will be loved only if you have sex with someone, but the gospel says you are worthy of love as you are. Maybe you have built an identity on the need to sexually conquer others, but the gospel says your true identity is in surrender to God's grace. Perhaps you have lived with bodily shame, but the gospel says Jesus's broken and crucified body has the power to heal the shame you carry.

THE PRACTICE OF SOBRIETY

A deeply formed sexual life is one marked by sobriety. By sobriety, I'm not referring to abstinence and willpower; I'm referring to honesty. In a given day, we are bombarded with temptations to objectify others. We emotionally use people to fill the loneliness we carry. We find ourselves in cycles of compulsive behavior that we think we can free ourselves from by greater willpower. When we find out yet again that we are in bondage, we hide from God and others until the guilt passes. We commit to trying harder and have marginal success. We then find ourselves vulnerable and led by our compulsions, and the cycle continues.

It's often been said that we are only as sick as our sickest secret. If this is the case, so many of us are riddled with illness and disease, and not just spiritually. When we hold on to secrets, our bodies often manifest the poison we've stored in our psyches. I'm reminded of the psalm that says, "When I kept silent, my bones wasted away through my groaning all day long" (32:3). The practice of sobriety is not just for people in drug or sex rehab programs; it's for all of us. Sobriety is intrinsically connected to truthfulness and transparency.

When we hold on to secrets, our bodies often manifest the poison we've stored in our psyches.

I acknowledge, sobriety as a practice is difficult. It asks us to lay down the false selves of strength we project onto the world. It invites us to live with poverty of spirit, nothing to prove, nothing to possess, and nothing to protect. It calls us to live free from the judgments and opinions of people. Some of the freest people are those with nothing to hide, yet being that way remains a gargantuan task, especially in the area of sexuality. How do we practice sobriety when our lives are marked by shame? I'd like to offer three ways forward.

Find a Sobriety Community

Every Monday, our church opens our doors for a Narcotics Anonymous group. The members are people who don't attend New Life but have found a community to be honest with. If you've ever been to an Alcoholics Anonymous or Narcotics Anonymous meeting, it is quite jarring and beautiful to hear the unbridled truth spoken from these men and women. There is something about the program that produces honesty and a spirit of sobriety. Having these meetings is not the only work that needs to be done, but without them, many cannot survive.

When I think about community life in many of our churches, I'm grieved that this kind of spirit is not to be found. This lack of sober community life actually reveals the power of shame that holds individuals and communities in bondage. Whatever we cannot name reveals our bondage to shame.

In the Harry Potter series, Voldemort, the evil villain and archenemy of Harry, has such a hold on everyone that just to say his name conjured fear and despair. Instead of saying his name, men, women, and children referred to him as You-Know-Who or He-Who-Must-Not-Be-Named. The only wizards who called Voldemort by his name were Harry and Dumbledore, and Harry would prove to be victorious over him. In the forging of honest communities, we release ourselves from the fearful shame that ruins our lives. We are given a gracious space to name what many say "must not be named." Sometimes this community is found in one other person—sometimes three or more. But the practice of sobriety is imperative in a world marked by sexual disorder and bondage.

Reframe Addiction

The practice of sobriety also requires us to reframe addiction. We find it hard to speak honestly about our addiction because we have fixated ourselves on the act and not on the pain the addiction is seeking to soothe. Addiction is our attempt to relieve ourselves from the unbearable pain of the moment. Whether it's food, pornography, incessant technological distraction, or drugs, the moment has become too overwhelming. We need an outlet. But the outlet further deepens our disordered lives.

However, before we preach against the ills of addictive behavior and such, we'd do well to appreciate one role that addiction can play in survival. I know that sounds blasphemous to some, but hear me out. Our addiction is our best attempt to survive. Certainly, it leads us down paths of sickness and death, but it is also a signal that we long to live. We just don't know how, apart from this attempt to self-soothe. This is why when helping someone with any kind of addiction, instead of saying, "Just stop it. Repent of your sin," we'd do better to say, "You've figured out how to stay alive. You've learned how to soothe your pain. But this way doesn't go deep enough. Let's try something else."

Confess Through Prayer

Every day I pray the Lord's Prayer. I need to pray it contemplatively for the sake of my own well-being. When I get to the portion that says, "Lead us not into temptation, but deliver us from evil" (Matthew 6:13), I'm reminded of the many weaknesses I have. That portion of the prayer doesn't mean that God leads us into temptation; rather, it is a confession of our weakness. It's us essentially saying, "Lord, I'm weak. I can't handle the pressure. I'm vulnerable. Don't put me to the test." In the words of author Dallas Willard, "It is a vote of 'no confidence' in our own abilities."[1]

When we pray confessional prayers regularly, we gain the proper perspective of our lives. We see ourselves in honesty and transparency before God, which is to be carried on to our relationships with others. This is why daily confession in prayer is essential to our lives. We repeatedly remind ourselves that we aren't as strong as we think. This is the heart of a sober person.

THE PRACTICE OF SOCIAL BONDING

In the previous chapter, we looked at Marva Dawn's analysis of Genesis 1 and 2. She distinguished genital sexuality from social sexuality. She made the important point that many people anxiously rush for genital sexuality when what they needed is social bonding and closeness. This is not to deny the biological and passionate fire that flows through our bodies, especially in moments of physical and romantic attraction (more on this later).

To absolutely deny the very real affection and longing we have is to subscribe to the starvation diet. This is not a good option. However, in our attempts to satisfy the longing for intimacy, connection, and vulnerability, we rush to the act of sex prematurely. In the process, we find ourselves spiritually and emotionally attached to others because we have given our bodies over without the protective gift of covenant vows. (I should clarify that just because someone is married doesn't automatically lead to intimacy, connection, and vulnerability.)

We should again return to Jesus as our example. Jesus, being fully God *and* fully human, understood the need for a social bonding. Jesus experienced intimacy, connection, and vulnerability throughout his life. He gathered disciples around him, feasted at parties, received love, confessed his weakness, revealed intimate details about himself, and gave and received tender physical touch. No one could say there was anything lacking in Jesus's humanity, even if he didn't experience genital sexuality.

When I mention practicing social bonding, I'm referring to the need to live connected to others in life-giving relationship. This is not exclusively for married people; this applies to singles as well. And this is needed in our day to fight the rampant force of loneliness.

The irony of our time is that we live in the most connected era in human history, yet we are lonelier than ever. Loneliness has become one of the greatest public-health challenges we experience. In 2018, Theresa May, who was prime minister of the United Kingdom at the time, recognized this problem and responded by appointing a loneliness minister. In her loneliness strategy, May said, "Loneliness is a reality for too many people in our society today. It can affect anyone of any age and background. Across our communities there are people who can go for days, weeks or even a month without seeing a friend or family member."[2] How is it that we can be surrounded by crowds of people and still feel lonely? How is it that we can have thousands of social media friends and follows but not truly be connected? The answer is simple: loneliness is combated not solely by physical proximity but by emotional closeness.

This is the essence of a spirituality of marriage to Christ. In the love relationship we have with Jesus, that intimate, vulnerable, connected love is to be expressed in concrete relationships as well. When I think about who does this well, I think about Sue. Sue is a single woman in her sixties who goes to our church and works as a therapist and spiritual-formation teacher. At some point on her faith journey, she received a wonderful vision for her life and what it meant to socially and emotionally bond with others. She sent the following to me in an email:

> For so many, singleness is the visible sign (stigma) of being "not chosen." It carries the pain of feeling unloved and unlovable, undesired and undesirable, lonely and alone. For many, it means a life lived in limbo, postponing or despairing of living a full life "until" marriage. I believe those are lies from the pit of hell, because they "steal, kill, and destroy" [see John 10:10], and Jesus came to give us abundant life marked by righteousness, peace, and joy in the Holy Spirit.
>
> As a single person married to Christ, I see, believe, and endeavor to live by these truths that have come alive to me as I've walked with Him. I hope they are visible in my life:
>
> - I am chosen. I do not belong to myself but to Christ who bought me with His own blood. I am His temple, and He deserves to be glorified in, with, and through me. This means that I am not preoccupied with myself. My life isn't all about me but Him.
>
> - I am loved, and His love and kindness drew me to Him. My love for Him is a response to His love for me. I know my-

self as beloved, and He is my beloved. There is a deep longing in me to see Him face to face, yet He has taught me to see Him in the eyes of the one before me. This translates into trying to be truly present to people, to live lovingly, to not use people, but to serve them for His sake. Being single gives me time and space to be available for whoever or whatever He sets before me. I have had so many opportunities for wonderful relationships and experiences because I've been free to engage them. I've known much joy and fulfillment in that freedom.

- Our marriage has brought me into His family. I am not alone. My love and loyalty to Him has made loving and serving His family a priority in my life, and I have been enriched by their love shown to me. When I became a Christian, my family turned away from me, but God sets the solitary in families (see Psalm 68:6), and I found a new family with His people. I have close relationships with other singles, as well as marrieds and families. I'm often included in their lives, but I've also initiated some of those relationships. I've never really identified as a single but as a person and fellow member of Christ's body. I don't think of singleness as a barrier but as an opportunity to connect.[3]

Sue offers a beautiful perspective for a world that has been alienated, even with greater technological connection at our disposal. The practice of social bonding is about the forging of intimate friendships—to know and be known. This certainly requires risk, a tolerance for awkwardness, and commitment to others, but for the sake of our flourishing as human beings, it is unquestionably necessary.

Practically speaking, social bonding is deepened as we progressively join or create opportunities for connection. This might be a small group that meets in a coffee shop, or a home-meal group. It might consist of a monthly outing with a friend or a season of therapy. However social bonding looks, we cannot go without it.

THE PRACTICE OF TOUCH

As we nurture our sexuality, we need to practice touch. Now, for some of you, this sounds great; for others, not so much. In my marriage to Rosie, I'm without question the "toucher." I want multiple hugs a day. When we are on the couch, my body finds a way to be close to hers. When in bed, my foot tends to drift over to her side. As I'm driving, I like to put my hand on her leg. My kids will attest to how many kisses and hugs I give them a day.

As a pastor, one of my favorite moments of the week is to shake hands and hug congregants in the lobby. I come from a family that touches as if there's a prize to be won. When I see my uncles, we exchange kisses on the cheek. When I see my aunts and cousins, there are long embraces to follow. However, my wife doesn't quite have the enthusiasm for touch that I do. My kids get a bit tired of the hugs. Some relatives just want a handshake and no more. Some congregants just give me a fist bump or end up giving me the awkward church side hug. But no matter where we are on the spectrum of touch, we all need it.

When a baby is born, the first thing doctors do is put the infant on the naked chest of her mother. This is the practice of skin-to-skin contact. Research has shown how this simple act regulates the infant in the new environment she finds herself in and ensures physical, emotional, and social development. Beyond the initial stages of infancy, however, we need healthy touch. We desire a physical closeness to others that is not marked by using, domination, or abuse. As human beings, we are sensual; that is, we have been given the gift of our senses to navigate the world well.

However, for many reasons, we live impaired in this area. Without journeying toward a life wherein healthy touch is pursued, we find ourselves living less-than-fully-human lives. In *The Body Keeps the Score,* Dr. Bessel van der Kolk told a story of a woman named Marilyn, a woman in her midthirties who worked as an operating-room nurse. Even though she tended to stay away from men, one day she met a fireman named Michael at a sports club. After many tennis matches over the course of time, she was comfortable enough to connect with Michael outside the sports setting. One Saturday evening, she invited him to stay over at her apartment:

> [Marilyn] described feeling "uptight and unreal" as soon as they were alone together. She remembered asking him to go slow but had

very little sense of what had happened after that. After a few glasses of wine and a rerun of *Law & Order,* they apparently fell asleep together on top of her bed. At around two in the morning, Michael turned over in his sleep. When Marilyn felt his body touch hers, she exploded—pounding him with her fists, scratching and biting, screaming, "You bastard, you bastard!" Michael, startled awake, grabbed his belongings and fled. After he left, Marilyn sat on her bed for hours, stunned by what had happened. She felt deeply humiliated and hated herself for what she had done, and now she'd come to me for help in dealing with her terror of men and her inexplicable rage attacks.[4]

After seeing Dr. van der Kolk, Marilyn faced the sexual-abuse trauma she'd experienced as a child. For Marilyn, being touched, especially by a man, triggered excruciatingly painful memories that were largely subconscious. Some of you reading this might identify with her story. Lately, there have been countless stories of damaging touch through the misuse of male power. I recognize the deep challenge before us. As a pastor, it does not escape me that thousands of people have been victims of abusive touch in the church. This is a grave sin that breaks God's heart and compromises our witness in the world. The act of healthy touch in church settings is profoundly needed and must be carefully discerned.

In addition to the many people who have lived with abusive touch, others have lived with an absence of touch. We see this in many stories of the New Testament where

Jesus came into contact with people who had been socially, emotionally, and religiously shunned because of the condition of their bodies. Whether it was leprosy, paralysis, or an issue of blood, to touch such people was to be regarded as ceremonially unclean. However, in Jesus, we see restoring of limbs and skin, hearing and sight, through gentle and subversive touch.

There were times when Jesus could just say a word from a distance and someone would be healed, but more often than not he laid his hands on the individual. In demonstrating the power of God through human touch, Jesus was not just healing a body; he was restoring community. This is what healthy touch does. This is why "virtual church" experiences will always be a poor substitute for physically gathering as the people of God. As we pass on peace to each other through handshakes, hugs, and kisses, we find something of our humanity touched and renewed. The practice of touch can be developed simply by showing up to church.

We practice touch as we pray for one another. As a matter of respecting the physical boundaries of others, I recommend asking for permission before placing hands on heads, shoulders, backs, and so on, especially when we don't know the person. But it can be a powerful act of healing when gentle hands of prayer are extended. It's a way of saying that God is not just with you in spirit but also with you in this moment through the act of touch.

I remember a moment in college when I was feeling quite lonely. Romantic relationships weren't working out, and I felt unattractive, depressed, and isolated. In one of the campus chapel services I attended, I remained seated with my eyes closed as the service ended. The worship team was still softly playing music on the platform when a professor I knew well came and placed his hands on my shoulders. He waited a short while before praying for me, but he didn't need to say a word. The simple act of touch reminded me that God saw me and had not forgotten me.

THE PRACTICE OF MAKING LOVE

Lovemaking takes practice—lots of it. In 2013, I met with a nationally known retired pastor in his midseventies. In our conversation, I asked him to share about his current season in life. He talked about the books he had read and written, the family he was enjoying, and his flourishing marriage. Before I asked him to elaborate further, he volunteered some information. He said, "My wife and I have been married more than fifty years, and we are having the best sex ever." I think my eyebrows furrowed as I gave him a side-eye. "Really?" I curiously responded. Without going into too much detail, he said, "It takes a lifetime to learn how to make love."

Lovemaking takes practice—lots of it.

Many fall for the myth that says genital sexual relations should be effortless, flawless, and "beyond this world." We have consumed these myths in the romantic comedies and dramas we watch, the novels we read, or the porn-saturated world we live. As one who was exposed to pornography at a very young age, I was formed to believe that the act of sexual intercourse should look like what I saw. I was shaped to see sex as a performance-driven, self-satisfying endeavor that went no deeper than my body parts. How destructive.

Lovemaking—if it is truly deeply formed—requires all our being. And this takes lots of practice. As I said earlier, the practice of lovemaking requires the protective context of covenant marriage. I recognize that this is not a popular (or some may say realistic) proposal. Like many people, I was sexually active as early as my teen years. I fully understand the fire that dwells within and the deep need to quench it. However, I also understand the emotional and spiritual damage that occurs when we give ourselves over to another without the presence of covenant vows. This notwithstanding, lovemaking takes practice, and it begins outside the bedroom.

Lovemaking Outside the Bedroom

When I say lovemaking outside the bedroom, I'm not referring to having sex in another part of the house (not a bad idea); I'm referring to the commitment to love each other outside the moment of sexual engagement. Lovemaking doesn't begin when we take our clothes off at night but rather when we put them on in the morning. As we demonstrate passion, curiosity, affirmation, playfulness, and the like, we create an atmosphere that doesn't reduce lovemaking to a particular act. I like how First Nations author Richard Wagamese put it:

> I don't want to touch you skin to skin. I want
> to touch you deeply, beneath the surface, where

our real stories lie. Touch you where the frag-
ments of our being are, where the sediment of
things that shaped us forms the verdant delta of
our human story. I want to bump against you
and feel the rush of contact and ask important
questions and offer compelling answers, so that
together we might learn to live beneath the surface, where the current bears us forward deeper
into the great ocean of shared experience. This
is how I want to touch and be touched—
through beingness—so that someday I might
discover that even the skin remembers.[5]

Wagamese beautifully expressed the connection we
yearn for "beneath the surface." This is the essence of
lovemaking outside the bedroom. In the acts of service,
spontaneous and carefully crafted words of appreciation,
tender touches, and intentional time spent together,
married couples expand lovemaking beyond the act of
intercourse. Intercourse is the climax of the often ordinary, sensual, clumsy, romantic ascent we take outside
the bedroom, and this takes practice.

Lovemaking doesn't begin when we take
our clothes off at night but rather when we
put them on in the morning.

As of the time of this writing, Rosie and I have been
married nearly fifteen years. I recognized that I wasn't
giving much thought to my lovemaking outside the bed-

room. (Rosie certainly hinted that there could be improvements.) As we were in our small kitchen, I asked her a couple of questions that I should have asked sooner: "Honey, when do you feel most loved by me? When do you feel closest to me?" She responded, "When we go out to a nice place and spend time together." That's not how I would have answered the question. But at that point, I once again had to shift my energy to love her in a way that she wanted to receive it.

Lovemaking Is Communication, Not an Activity

It's quite easy to think of sexual intercourse as just an activity. But it's more than that—much more. Sex is something you say, not just something you do. In the act of sex, you are communicating to each other. You are fostering an environment of communion that encompasses the moment of intercourse. In practicing lovemaking, we move outside performance-oriented self-preoccupation.

Lovemaking is external in this regard. Something is being communicated from me to my spouse. I'm reminding my wife that she is loved and lovable. I'm communicating that she is seen and known. I'm expressing that she is treasured and appreciated. When sex is reduced to the moment, our lives with each other become transactional and potentially objectifying. When it is seen as simply an act, our spouses' bodies become means to an end and we are in danger of having marriages shaped by using and not communion.

As part of the communication, lovemaking requires us to be honest about our preferences, likes, dislikes, and the rest. Lovemaking, whether in the bedroom or outside it, requires clear articulation of how we desire to receive and give love. We must learn to be honest with how we feel about our partners' desires. Lovemaking is damaged when we have to resort to mind reading and imposing our preferences on another. In this respect, lovemaking is risky because it requires honesty and vulnerability to share what is desired and preferred. There are times when those desires might not be met exactly how we want. This is why lovemaking takes practice. As we tenderly share what we desire, we are able to love each other as we are and not as we wish we were. Remember the words of the pastor I quoted a few pages back: "It takes a lifetime to learn how to make love."

Lovemaking Is a Revelation

Lovemaking in and outside the bedroom is a revelation. What does it reveal? Well, without overstating it, it reveals God. It is sacramental. Our lovemaking is to manifest our union with each other and, in so doing, manifest God's union with the world.

In this way, lovemaking is eucharistic. Through the bread and cup, Jesus offered us his body. "Take, eat and drink, this is my body, given for you," he said (see Luke 22:19–20). Because we are deeply formed people seeking to follow Jesus, our lovemaking reveals God's love to each other. As we love each other, naked and unashamed, we enact the vulnerable, free, faithful, and fruitful qualities of love demonstrated in Jesus. He would lay down his life for us, give his body for us, pronounce forgiveness and grace, and renew us through this self-giving love. This too is what deeply formed sex is. It is the holy demonstration of God's naked and unashamed love toward us.

Moreover, lovemaking is an act of mission. When a

couple is in love—giving and receiving each other in bodily, emotional, and spiritual communion—they can't help but overflow in love to the world around them. I'm most happy, joyful, content, and generous when my wife and I are living from a place of loving union with each other. On the other hand, I'm not nearly as happy, joyful, content, and generous when we are not living from that place. It sounds strange to say, but we are at our best when we are making love, inside and outside the bedroom.

The practices I offer are not exhaustive by any means, but I believe they capture some of the significant areas of our lives that lead to sexual wholeness. Wherever you find yourself on the journey today, know that God is gracious. He knows we are from dust. Christ knows our weaknesses, as he was human himself. The Spirit resides in us to comfort and strengthen us. The body of Christ exists to be the presence of Jesus on earth. You are not alone. God has the power to redeem all things.

NINE

Missional Presence in a Distracted and Disengaged World

In his classic autobiography *The Seven Storey Mountain*, Thomas Merton recounted an experience he had with a simple yet mysterious Hindu man who lived a monastic life. In his conversation with the man, known as Brahmachari, they discussed the effect of Christian missionaries in parts of South Asia. Brahmachari noted that Christian missionaries had minimal impact in that part of the world for many reasons. Chiefly, they weren't holy enough. As Merton reflected on this significant conversation, he concluded that "the Hindus are not looking for us to send them men who will build schools and hospitals, although those things are good and useful in themselves—and perhaps very badly needed in India: they want to know if we have any saints to send them."[1]

"They want to know if we have any saints to send them."

As I read that line, I was reminded that any talk of being engaged in the world must begin not with activity but with a life in God. The Hindus in this story were looking for people who could model a different way of being in the world. It's not that the work projects don't matter. We need them. What matters more is the quality of lives out of which the work flows. Our lives are to be joined with God in love, in contemplation, in surrender, in obedience, and out of that, in loving service and mission to the world.

Over the course of our three decades, our church has sought to regularly wrestle with the tension between monastery and mission. We are not called to remain within cloistered walls, giving ourselves to prayer apart from social engagement with the world. Nor are we called to perpetually and indiscriminately be consumed with being active in the world. We are called to hold this dynamic tension before God. Why? Very simply, unless we do so, we have nothing to offer the world.

Do we have any saints to send?

BEING JESUS FOR ANOTHER

When I speak of deeply formed mission, I'm connecting all of what we've learned together in this book. There is a way of responding to the needs of the world in such a way that leads to fatigue and burnout. We try to give what we don't possess, and every time we attempt this, we put ourselves in danger. Is there a way to actively respond to the injustice, poverty, and pain that people experience without being destroyed by our good intentions and deeds? I think we can. But a shift is required. The deeply formed mission is fundamentally about becoming a particular person and offering that to the world. This kind of mission is not just about activity; it's about being Christ for another.

Anyone who belongs to Jesus is indwelled by his Spirit. This indwelling life is not simply for the purpose of private, mystical experiences; it's also for the purpose of being shared with the world around us. Some of you reading this are already tuning me out. Perhaps you look at your life and think, *I can never be Jesus—I can't even find my Bible; my prayer life is so inconsistent; I have too many sins that need forgiving; I just became a Christian, so how can I be Jesus for another?* or *I don't feel close to God.*

Deeply formed mission is first about *who* we are becoming before *what* we are doing. Our most effective strategy in reaching a world for Christ is grounded in the kind of people we are being formed into. The quality of our presence is our mission. And the good news is that Jesus doesn't wait for us to be perfect before inviting us into mission. On the contrary, being "perfect" disqualifies us from partnering with Jesus in mission. When you read the Bible, you'll see again and again that God doesn't call perfect people. I recall a humorous line from Homer Simpson. Upon reading the Bible, he says, "Everybody's a sinner . . . except for this guy."[2] He, of course, has Jesus in mind.

Deeply formed mission is first about *who* we are becoming before *what* we are doing.

God is in the business of calling broken, fearful, hotheaded, inconsistent, pessimistic, doubting people like you and me. That's what makes the gospel good news. Just look at Jesus's first disciples.

As Jesus was arrested and crucified, his disciples deserted him. He was left alone to suffer and die. After his death, burial, and resurrection, the disciples locked themselves in a room for fear that they would be next to die. These disciples had failed Jesus. They'd dropped out. Who would want these people on their team? The answer is no one except Jesus. Jesus went back to his failed disciples and instead of bringing up their mistakes, he sent them on mission. After coming face to face with his friends, he said, "Peace be with you. As the Father has sent me, even so I am sending you." And after he said this, "he breathed on them and said to them, 'Receive the Holy Spirit'" (John 20:21–22). This is the good news of the gospel. Even when you make mistakes, don't perform, and can't get your act together, Jesus comes to you and says, "I want you. I'm calling you, and I'm sending you." Jesus knows your problems, your addictions, your hang-ups, and your failures, and in spite of that, you are invited into his mission.

The missional task of being Jesus for others is open to all who would follow him, but I would be misleading you if I told you it didn't cost you anything. To say yes to this invitation requires you to surrender a way of being on mission that compartmentalizes doing from being. In some Christian traditions, doing is often at the expense of being. In others, being is often at the expense of doing. We need a life of doing that flows from being. Before I go there, I want to take a moment to address both of these extremes.

Doing Without Being

As I mentioned before, many of the Evangelical and Pentecostal traditions that have shaped me tend to place an
inordinate amount of emphasis on right thinking, right
experiences, and right doing. Regarding the "doing"
part, the approach to mission is often compartmentalized. Certainly, there's much to be done and many are in
need, but the gravitational pull of doing at the expense of
being does more damage in the long run. This reminds
me of a conversation I had with Pete Scazzero during my
job interview for a pastoral position.

During the final interview, Pete sat across a table piled
with fries and grilled cheese sandwiches and said to me
(in what I thought was hyperbolic language), "Rich,
there's only one way to get fired at this church." I sat up
straight, waiting for him to give an example of some kind
of gross moral failure. He said, "If you don't keep Sabbath, you will get fired because you won't have the kind
of life that will sustain you for the type of work pastoring
entails." I was jolted and puzzled, but his point was clear.
Any *doing* on our part will be only as deep as our *being*.
To do without being might look the same to an outsider,
but the quality of our lives is drastically different. To do
without being disconnects our activity from the source of
life and love: God's life and love.

When we're doing without being, we're liable to serve
in order to gain the approval of others, lead to mask a
deep sense of insecurity, volunteer to get God to love us
more, start new things to prove our worth, and over-
function, not giving adequate space for our own health.

The list goes on. Sooner or later the consequences of doing without being catch up to us, whether in the form of sickness, resentment, duplicity, or fatigue. Our engagement in the world becomes marked by a kind of stale obligation rather than joyful participation.

The remedy for this kind of missional engagement is not *total* withdrawal but *creative* withdrawal. In the soul-creating moments of being with God and others, the quality of our lives overflows to reach others. This is something we constantly have to keep before us in our local congregation.

Simply put, you can't give what you haven't received.

New Life is a significantly active church. As I mentioned earlier, our Community Development Corporation serves thousands of poor and overlooked families in our neighborhood. We have many small groups that have been places of healing and hospitality to the unchurched. We have large outreaches and help our congregation hold the connection between faith and work. We have a history of church planting and are reimagining what empowering leaders and starting new churches can look like in our day.

We are deeply engaged in our city. But we have been reminded regularly that our doing must flow from our being. Why? Simply put, you can't give what you haven't received.

Being Without Doing

The gravitational pull of being with God at the expense of doing for and with God is very real. In our congregation, we have both sides of the coin. Some people are very engaged but don't prioritize being with God. Others prioritize being with God but aren't engaged in doing.

One of the challenges we've had to repeatedly address at our church is the influx of people from other churches who are burned out, looking for a place of respite. Many people in the New York area see our church as an emotionally healthy church. Consequently, if you need a place for Sabbath, self-care, and recovery, this is the place to go. Well, in our history, many people swing the pendulum in a direction that goes from workaholism to being allergic to being on mission.

Certainly, there are seasons for recovery, rest, and disengagement, but there is to be an interplay at work. We are not to be Mary to the exclusion of Martha, nor are we to be Martha at the exclusion of Mary (see Luke 10:38–42). We are called to be active contemplatives or contemplative activists, holding together the invitation to be and to do. This is what we see with the God revealed in Scripture. The invitation to deeply formed mission is one that starts with the liberating understanding that he is always on mission but from a place of being. From the quality of God's life, God acts.

A MISSIONARY GOD

There is never a moment when God isn't moving toward the world in love. The psalmist says that God doesn't slumber or sleep (see 121:4). But even God's mission flows from his being. To describe this God who is always in motion from being, it's helpful to explore an important theological word, *perichoresis*, which was introduced by the Cappadocian Fathers of the fourth century. This word describes the metaphor of an eternal dance of love between Father, Son, and Holy Spirit. Scripture reveals a God-in-community, lovingly dancing in attentive relationship.

There is never a moment when God isn't moving toward the world in love.

But rather than being an insular dance that others stand outside of, God's dance widens the circle of divine love. This is a helpful way to frame the conversation on how God is on mission. He is not on mission in a linear, arbitrary manner. In perpetual motion, he widens the circle of loving union, inviting us and all of creation into it. His very being is intrinsically connected with his very doing. German theologian Jürgen Moltmann, in *The Trinity and the Kingdom,* further explored this:

> An eternal life process takes place in the triune God through the exchange of energies. The

Father exists in the Son, the Son in the Father, and both of them in the Spirit, just as the Spirit exists in both the Father and the Son. By virtue of their eternal love they live in one another to such an extent, and dwell in one another to such an extent, that they are one. It is a process of most perfect and intense empathy. Precisely through the personal characteristics that distinguish them from one another, the Father, the Son and the Spirit dwell in one another and communicate eternal life to one another. In the perichoresis, the very thing that divides them becomes that which binds them together.[3]

Whenever my large extended family gets together, at some point in our gathering someone will play the famous song for the Electric Slide, which is a group dance that often gradually enlarges as people pay attention to the dance floor. Sometimes it starts with just one person, and just like that, within a matter of moments the rest of the party joins in. When I think of God as Trinity, this is what comes to mind. From all eternity, God has been dancing. But the kind of dance he engages in is not one in which an audience simply admires from a distance; it's the kind that everyone is invited to step into.

When you read the Bible in this light, it offers a compelling image for seeing God at work in mission. God dances and invites people throughout history to move in accordance with his rhythm of love. But sometimes we're off rhythm.

MY FIRST MISSION FIELD

After becoming a Christian, I was filled with a joy that could not be extinguished. Beyond joy, I was filled with an urgency to save everyone I could from a life without connection to God. As I stated in the introduction, I became a Christian in a Pentecostal church. In this context, two things were important: having a charismatic experience with the Holy Spirit and telling people about Jesus. Being the young nineteen-year-old that I was, I had enough zeal for the whole church. I was going to spread the good news, even at work.

The year after I became a Christian, I went through a temp agency to find work for a few months before going away to college. I was grateful to land a job in Union Square, Manhattan, for a small publishing company. I worked in the office-services department. From day one I was plotting how I could have conversations about faith with my coworkers. I was assigned a small cubicle, but because of my role, many people came to my area requesting office supplies. After a few days on the job, I had an idea. I thought, *What if I put a Bible verse on my screen saver? That might generate some conversation.*

Being the new Christian, I went right for the jugular. In bright-pink font with a green background, I put these words from Romans 3:23 using a font size of 120: "For all have sinned and fall short of the glory of God." That's it—nothing else. I was sure this would generate conversation. Well, it did. My supervisor, a woman in her midthirties who typically locked herself in her office, passed by my desk. I could see her looking puzzled as she silently mouthed the words on my computer screen.

With an aloof smile that would have made Michael Scott from *The Office* cringe, I asked how she was doing, anticipating a moment of revival in my office space. After a few words, she left my cubicle, only to come back ten minutes later.

"Rich, you can't have language like this on the computer screen. It's offensive. Please take it down."

Insulted by her words, I argued that this was *my* cubicle. (Remember, I was a nineteen-year-old Christian zealot at the time.) She repeated her initial command. I took my message down. I went home that day to strategize how I could spread the word to the office the next day. At home, probably watching some Christian-television station, I had another idea: I would wear a T-shirt with Bible verses on it to work. Since becoming a Christian, I had at least four of these shirts. The next day I walked into the office wearing the word of God. *Ha! She can't tell me to take my shirt off.*

My supervisor saw my shirt and again I smiled, this time with a look of victory. She took a deep breath and locked herself back in her office. For the few months that I worked there, I didn't have too many healthy conversations on faith. I somehow thought that people needed to be debated into the kingdom. On the final day of my temp job, I decided that the only way I could preach to the entire company was to send a mass email. So I did.

I told them they were all sinners in need of salvation. I closed my three-paragraph email with the sinner's prayer, hit send, and walked out of the building as though I owned the joint. I wouldn't be surprised if I'm on a prohibited list in that building (nor would I blame them).

When we think of being on mission, some of us believe we need this level of aggressiveness to make a difference. Yet there is a better way—much better. God is in the business of rescuing people. We are all called to play a part in facilitating this salvation, but in ways that bear witness to the loving winsomeness of Jesus. What, then, is deeply formed mission? In short, deeply formed mission refers to the presence, posture, and pervasiveness of our witness to Jesus in our world. But our mission is shaped by *missio Dei,* God's mission in the world. It's along these lines that I want to explore two missional facets that are to shape our lives: God with all, and God for all.

GOD WITH ALL: MISSIONAL PRESENCE

Any sense of mission that is faithful to Jesus begins with the presence of God. God's grace is lovingly present to the world at every moment. That's not to say that his presence is easy to discern. It's often difficult to locate the presence of God or believe that he is near, especially in hard moments, but theologically there's no place where he is not at work. Jesus said, "My Father is always at his work to this very day" (John 5:17, NIV). It's quite comforting to me that God doesn't take days off. Although we all have limits, God does not. He is with us. Any notion of mission in this world must confess that God moves first. Long before we act, God has already acted. Long before we speak, God has already spoken. Long before we arrive, God has been present.

The story of the Bible is the story of God's presence with his people. A brief survey of the biblical story line depicts a God who is never without a people. From the opening pages of Scripture, God creates humanity, fashioning them in a garden. But he doesn't settle them in and leave them on their own. God, in the cool of the day, walks among his people. Even when they sin and are banished from the Garden of Eden, he still reaches out, looking to restore communion and relationship.

Throughout the Hebrew scriptures, God repeatedly shows up in history, taking the initiative to dwell among his people. He comes as a pillar of fire and a cloud to guide his people through the desert in the book of Exodus. God took up residence in a tabernacle, seeking relationship with his wandering covenant community. Later on, he instructed his people to establish a more permanent place of dwelling in the form of a temple. In the Holy of Holies, God's presence dwelled. But that too came to an end. The people of God, as a result of their rebellion and sin, found themselves exiled in a faraway land. But even there, God would raise up prophets to speak to his people. Throughout the Old Testament, God is dwelling with a people.

This theme is taken further in the New Testament. In the opening pages of each gospel account, we read the stunning news that God has taken up residence yet again. This time it's not in a cloud, fire, tabernacle, or temple or through the words of a prophet. In Jesus, God comes to dwell among God's people. God can't get enough of us. From Genesis to Revelation, we come across a God who refuses to be without a people. God comes to be present and available, offering unlimited love to the world.

All of this has implications for our engagement with our neighbors and the surrounding world. If God is present, our fundamental call is to be present as well. Yet this is easier said than done. One of the anxieties people carry when thinking about engaging in mission is the pressure to get another to cross the line of salvation. As a result, many Christians have seen people as projects to fix instead of relationships to nurture. Being on mission is often awkward, coercive, and unnatural because our fixation with getting someone to a "decision" reduces that person to that decision. Furthermore, some Christians have been formed to engage the world in mission through guilt and fear, as opposed to grace and mercy. When our lives are fixated on a particular outcome, we lose our ability to be truly present.

The Evangelistic projects undertaken by some often come across as self-protection and works-righteousness. We are made to think that if we don't get these people to the point of decision, *we* will be judged by God. When fear of judgment serves as the motivation to get others to make a decision, we have ceased to be on mission in Jesus's way. This is not to say that we aren't to carry a sense of urgency. Not at all. I believe that faith in Jesus and following the way of his kingdom lead to the kind of life everyone truly longs for. I have a deep desire for people to know of God's self-giving love and to embody that love in the world. The world longs for this. However, the way we get there is not through anxious, coercive, sanctified guilt trips. How, then, shall we be on mission? Well, we can start by creating space for presence.

I wholeheartedly believe that God has already begun a

conversation with someone long before I arrive. If it is true, as Paul declares in Acts 17:28, that in God "we live and move and have our being," every person on the face of this planet is already, on some level, being encountered by God. The individual might not be able to cognitively perceive it or receive it, but Christian theology assumes God's active presence all over the world. What's needed is for Christ followers to discern God's presence rather than assuming his absence.

We'll often think, *God can't be with those Democrats... with those Republicans... with those in the local bar... in the mosque... at the Gay Pride parade,* and on and on it goes. We too often assume God's absence. We are formed to believe that God is only with people and in places that mirror our belief systems. Or we believe he is present in supernatural spiritual moments but not in the ordinary moments of our lives. I'm regularly guilty of this.

One day I wrote a prayer in my journal that said, "Lord, today I'm reminded that I'm part of a great story that is developing over thousands of years. You are making all things new. You are restoring the world to yourself, and you are inviting me to join you in this work. Send me to whomever you want. I want to be present to others as you are."

As I wrote and prayed these words, my daughter (who was four years old at the time) asked me to pour her a bowl of cereal. I took her request as an annoying distraction. How dare she interrupt my time with God! After all, I was asking him to help me join him in remaking the world.

After begrudgingly pouring cereal, I went back to pray. Then it hit me, and I felt conviction in my heart:

The act of being lovingly present to her at that moment was a small act of remaking the world. It was unimpressively simple and yet core to what it means to follow Jesus. Here's how my journal entry ended: "Lord, I've looked at this basic request of cereal as a distraction, yet joining you in the restoration of the world must include pouring milk and Cheerios for a little girl. Teach me to be lovingly present to my family and anyone you put in my path today. Amen." Over and over I've found these words easy to pray but so hard to live.

GOD FOR ALL: MISSIONAL POSTURE

God is for the world, period. This truth makes or breaks our understanding of mission. To deny this assertion is to see God in a fundamentally different light than the light revealed in Jesus. Yet that different light is the default mode of much of Christianity. We are often known for what we are against rather than what we are for. A simple test will confirm this to be true. Bring up any divisive issue in our world—politics, sexuality, race, immigration, and so on—and what you'll find are Christians clearly asserting what they are against. But any conversation regarding the nature of God must begin with him being *for* all. Mission for a Christian must begin not with human fallenness but with God's posture toward the world.

When we see people with a "Make America Great Again" hat, we can see them from a posture of God's commitment toward them or from the perspective of our own boundary making. When we see a woman of color with a #blacklivesmatter T-shirt, we can see her through the lens of God's heart of mercy toward her or reduce her entire humanity to a hashtag. When we see an immigrant, we can see him through the lens of God's tender love or through the lens of fearful scape-goating.

God's posture toward the world is always for us: "God so loved the world, that he gave his only Son" (John 3:16). This is the definitive Bible verse declaring God's committed love toward us. By entering into human his-tory, God made a very clear declaration, saying in effect, "I don't want to exist without you." Does God exist without us? Of course. Does God *want* to exist without us? Not a chance. God is for us. This is the foundation of mission.

How can mission that is consistent with Jesus be es-tablished on the grounds of judgment, disgust, and "oth-ering"? Actually, it can't. Missional presence takes on the posture of the God and Father revealed in Jesus. God didn't need creation or company, but out of divine gen-erosity, he brought creation into existence not to subject it to bondage but to have it feast at the table of goodness.

To affirm that God is for us is to confess with clarity who is *us*. If by *us* we mean fellow Christians—especially those who believe as we do—then that *us* is much too confined. The *us* that God is for always extends to all people and to the entirety of creation.

A WORLD OF PEOPLE SET
AGAINST ONE ANOTHER

Our world is often marked by a level of such hostility, animus, and vitriol that compassion feels like impossible reality. As Mother Teresa famously stated, "If you judge people, you have no time to love them."[4] The attacking that permeates our souls and cities is fueled by deep fear and suspicion. The posture of being against the world is one that has marked Christian witness for centuries, but what makes genuine Christian engagement with the world different is that we don't hate the people we are trying to change.

This takes a profound work of the Holy Spirit in our lives because we are formed to be against. On any given day, we are confronted with news stories that thrive off antagonisms.

LIVING AS SENT PEOPLE

As Jesus is sent by the Father, he sends his followers into the world as well. And Jesus's sending is gracious. He sends us as his representatives, his heralds, his ambassadors. One of the greatest acts of grace is Jesus calling his first disciples—and every disciple since then—into mission. But it's a mission informed by God's mission, shaped by God's action, and sustained by God's gracious initiative.

Deeply formed mission is not about activity for the sake of activity. Deeply formed mission joins together our being and our doing, seeing our presence, posture, and pervasiveness of mission as foundational to following Jesus.

In the next chapter, I will highlight four areas of deeply formed mission. These areas, like the redwood root system, must be integrated as we seek to witness to Jesus's kingdom in the twenty-first century. I'll explore the deeply formed missional practices of hospitality, commissioning our work, justice, and gospel proclamation, as well as consider the missional *space* of our workplaces.

TEN

Deeply Formed Practices
of Missional Presence

On a hot Sunday afternoon several years ago, I painfully observed a zealous believer attempting to share his Christian faith on a city bus. I had preached three services at church and decided to take the bus home. I had my son with me, who was nine months old. Nathan was a chunky baby, and I carried him in one of those bucket infant car seats. When the bus pulled up, I loaded Nathan and myself onto it, appreciating the cool air-conditioning, and took a seat toward the back. I put Nathan (still in the baby carrier) on the empty seat next to me, looked at him, and started to playfully interact with him. It was such a delightful afternoon.

At that moment, just a few feet behind me, I started hearing a gregarious man greeting everyone on the bus as if he were the mayor. Virtually no one greeted him in return. A few seconds later, he took out a big Bible and started to preach, quoting nonexistent Bible verses while passionately pointing to the words on the pages. My eyes began to roll. He then sensed the Spirit leading him to say that the bus was filled with sin, and I responded by taking deep breaths.

He shared his version of the gospel to a visibly annoyed "congregation" of about fifteen people, and as he did so, an older White woman interrupted his sermon and in no uncertain terms told him to shut up. He preached louder. She began cussing him out, so he started speaking in tongues. The people on the bus moved their heads back and forth like this was all playing out at a tennis match. She cursed. He spoke in tongues. She ridiculed him. He rebuked her. This went on for a solid minute (an eternity for me). After this exchange, they both settled down, and a soothing silence ensued.

Then, out of nowhere, the conversation turned. The cursing lady began to aim her rage at the Obama administration. She began preaching about the ills of socialism, to which the Christian preacher started saying amen. The people around us looked befuddled. I rubbed my forehead in exasperation.

Thirty seconds later, an older Black woman near me came to the defense of President Obama. "You better watch your mouth, lady!" she said. The two of them started getting into it. I live only two miles from the church, but this ten-minute ride felt as though it had doubled in time. Three or four people on the bus were now arguing when I decided to stand up. In my irritation, I proceeded to step off the bus a good five blocks before my stop, switching the car seat from hand to hand, struggling to carry my son. Another New York City moment.

Granted, this kind of public preaching has its place in some contexts, but this person seemed to be out of touch with the moment and with his method. Unlike this guy, however, many people experience some form of anxiety when it comes to expressing the faith they have come to believe in, and with good reason. We have often thought that being on mission means having to share our faith with strangers in some random location. We have incorrectly understood extroversion to be a spiritual gift that everyone must cultivate. But we need not think that this is what we signed up for. To be on mission is a multifaceted endeavor. God invites us to consider our personalities, context, and experiences and, out of who we are, discerningly participate in what he is already doing. Being on mission doesn't require us to be intrusive, awkward, and coercive. It should be a normal experience.

In this chapter, I want to name some practices to give expression to the good news of the gospel. To take the call of following Jesus seriously means we open ourselves up to the surrounding world, prayerfully moving toward it in love. The results are up to God, but we have a part to play.

When I think of words to describe deeply formed mission, I have in mind such words as *patience, empathy, curiosity, discernment, incarnational, noncoercive, invitational, justice,* and *service.* We need these words to combat a way of doing mission that is often impatient, transactional, coercive, obtrusive, judgmental, disembodied, and anxious. To this end, I want to invite you to consider a few ways forward. These four practices are both individual and communal, and they need to be. We bear witness to the good news of the gospel using both methods.

THE PRACTICE OF HOSPITALITY

Throughout the New Testament, Jesus demonstrated hospitality. In the ancient Near East, hospitality was a cultural norm, but Jesus transcended the norm. You see, hospitality is not simply the opening of our homes; it is the opening of our hearts to another. In Matthew 8, Jesus said, "Foxes have dens and birds have nests, but the Son of Man has no place to lay his head" (verse 20, NIV). Because of his itinerant ministry, Jesus was constantly on the move, yet he was the most hospitable person the world has seen.

In the next chapter, Matthew 9, Jesus created space to welcome and connect with people considered outsiders. Matthew, a newly called disciple of Jesus, joyfully opened his home to his fellow tax-collector and sinner friends (see verses 9–13). It was a wonderful idea. Matthew wanted to get his friends to connect with Jesus. What I love about this story is that Matthew and Jesus were offering hospitality in that moment. Matthew opened his home; Jesus opened his heart. In order to practice hospitality as mission, it requires us to do the same. Hospitality requires a posture of welcome. It's a way of saying, "You belong here." It's a way of saying, "It is good that you are here."

What's interesting in all this is that the people who Jesus was at the table with were considered outsiders. Jesus was eating with tax collectors. The religious Jewish community during that time despised tax collectors for many reasons. For one, no one likes to pay money to the government, especially when the government is an oppressive regime like the Roman Empire of the first century. Those who collected the taxes for such a government were despised by the people.

Another reason that tax collectors were despised was because many were Jews who were working for the hated Romans. These individuals were seen as traitors to their own countrymen. Rather than fighting the Roman oppressors, the tax collectors were helping them—and enriching themselves at the expense of their fellow Jews. Third, it was common knowledge that the tax collectors cheated the people they collected from. It was a normal practice for tax collectors to collect more than required and keep the extra for themselves. Everyone understood that was how it worked.

This is why Jesus was so scandalous. He had the nerve to touch those who were known to be contagious (lepers) and sit with people who were regarded as corrupt (tax collectors). The grace of Jesus knows nothing of the limited categories we project onto God. Those who are seen as questionable—whether through their morality or belief systems—are welcomed by Jesus. Jesus opens himself to those who are deemed far from God. Curiously, the only ones who have a hard time finding a place of welcome are those who have rejected others. Or to put it another way, the person who might be farthest from God might be the person who thinks others are too far from God. Jesus is safe enough for these people to approach him. He makes space.

A few years ago, I spent two days in Phoenix, speaking to pastors and leaders. Throughout the weekend, I had to take a few Uber rides to get around. For one of the trips, a woman in her early thirties picked me up. We started talking about why I was in Phoenix, and I told her I was a pastor. I asked her if she attended church, and she said, "I've created my own path: I'm spiritual." I asked her to elaborate. She told me that she takes truths from different religions and lives accordingly. So I asked her how it was working for her and if her path was leading to deep joy and fulfillment. She didn't have a clear answer.

I then asked her about Jesus. "Who is Jesus to you?" I asked. She said, "I've never thought about it." We continued to talk, and she continued to share her custom-made belief system as I listened. She began to kind of apologize for not giving a good answer about Jesus. I told her I just wanted to hear her story.

She mentioned that it is rare for a Christian to ask questions without judging her belief system, and she opened up some more. She started telling me about why her mother didn't go to church. At one point in her life, the family was struggling financially. Her mother went to the pastor of her church to ask for financial support. The pastor proceeded to look at her financial-giving record. In no uncertain terms, he told this mother that she couldn't withdraw funds if she wasn't giving anything.

I could sense the resentment in my driver's voice. By the end of the conversation, it became a bit clearer to me what was happening. Even though it was her car that I had entered into, I had an opportunity to practice hospitality. She was experiencing a sense of welcome. I don't know what happened next in her life, but I do know this: the more we create spaces for people who don't look like us, think like us, or believe like us, the more we will be able to introduce them to Jesus.

I'm reminded of an act of hospitality shown by some members of our church that was featured in the *New*

York Times. In 2014, there was some controversy in our part of the city. Evidently, there was a decision to convert an abandoned hotel into a shelter for 180 homeless families. The dilemma: the decision was made by the mayor's office without the input of local residents. This infuriated many of the residents, leading them to protest in front of the new homeless facility.

The problem was that their anger and indignation were aimed at the families (with many young children) living there. One could understand the frustration of the community, but just days after arriving into this new neighborhood, the new residents were made to feel as if they were not welcome. Ironically, the majority of protesters themselves came from immigrant backgrounds, yet for many reasons, they refused to extend welcome.

Upon hearing of this protest, a few New Life teenagers decided to offer an alternative approach. They were seeing these new residents as people made in the image of God who were deserving of welcome. Tala—a nineteen-year-old Pakistani young adult whose family immigrated to the United States when he was four—led a team to coordinate a barbecue for families in our church parking lot. Many people came and were joyfully received.[1]

The reason we are hospitable is to open our hearts to others in the way God has opened his heart to us.

Hospitality is a holy act because it mirrors the God who welcomes and receives all. As people deeply formed by this God, we are called to extend that grace to others, whether they are immigrants, refugees, new neighbors, or spiritually curious people. Of course, from a public-policy perspective, this doesn't mean that notions of hospitality and welcome delegitimize important factors related to security and such. But if we implicitly see someone as a threat, we will build walls to eliminate any semblance of that person's presence.

The deeply formed life is one that creates space for others. Whether that space is at our work right in our cubicles, with families at parks, or through opening our homes to others, we cannot be deeply formed into the image of Jesus without our lives mirroring gracious hospitality.

In the practice of hospitality, the goal is not to convert anyone (as if we could). The objective is not to corner someone and obtrusively preach at him or her. The reason we are hospitable is to open our hearts to others in the way God has opened his heart to us. I have found that as spaces are created, conversations on faith naturally emerge. As theologian Henri Nouwen said, "Hospitality is not to change people, but to offer them space where change can take place."[2]

THE PRACTICE OF JUSTICE

You might be wondering how justice can be a practice. If so, you're not alone. The work of justice is often relegated to people who have a particular bent toward making things right, but it should not be so. We are all called to practice justice. Practicing justice is an act of joining

God in seeing that the created order (people and everything else) receives what it is due. And we all have a penchant for justice. It's in our genes.

We are all hardwired to care about justice. One of my daughter's favorite things to say since she was three or four years old is "That's not fair." Granted, much of her cries of unfairness were not based on some kind of virtuous altruism (they were more like, "I want more ice cream"); however, like many children, she's able to name that which is not right. And she's not alone. Along these lines, I found an article that spoke to this, titled "That's Not Fair! Crime and Punishment in a Preschooler's Mind."

We are all hardwired to care about justice.

According to the article, by the age of three, kids actually "have a burgeoning sense of fairness and are inclined to right a wrong."[3] Additionally, when they see someone being mistreated, children as young as three years old will intervene on behalf of others nearly as often as for themselves. The author of the article described an experiment that verified this justice gene in children.

Researchers in the United Kingdom and Germany acted as puppeteers to learn when children develop their sense of justice and interest in punishment. The study included 137 children who were either three or five years old and involved each in several different scenarios. In one experiment, a devious puppet stole cookies that were originally intended for the child. In another, an innocent puppet cried out in distress when its marbles were snatched by a troublemaker puppet. The researchers watched the kids' reactions.

It turned out that the children weren't just concerned about their own precious cookies or toys; they would jump in to assist the wronged puppets too. Given the opportunity, three-year-olds would intervene to return items a puppet had stolen to the original owner nearly 60 percent of the time. They would take back their own stolen items almost 80 percent of the time.[4]

Even though from an early age we are inclined toward justice, for far too many it's not something that's actively practiced. Our excuses are numerous and varied: justice is for extroverted activist types, is for people who want to publicly protest, is not a gospel issue, or is restricted to divisive and national issues. The list goes on.

In truth, justice is a necessity for our world to reflect the good news of God's reign over all things. How, then, do we practice it? Before going there, let me offer some biblical framing of the term *justice*. Usually when we think of it, we tend to limit it to the courtroom. Justice in our culture tends to be limited to punishing criminals for bad deeds. When someone does something wrong and is convicted for it, we say, "Justice has been served." On the other side, when someone gets away with something, we call that a miscarriage of justice.

But biblical justice is more than punishment of wrongdoing. The Hebrew word for justice is *mishpat*. Although the meaning of this word in Scripture includes the punishment of wrongdoing, it predominantly means giving people what they are due as human beings made in the image of God. In the words of pastor and apologist Tim

Keller, *mishpat* "is giving people what they are due, whether punishment or protection or care."[5]

The latter two words of that meaning of justice, protection and care, are at the very heart of God. In Scripture, we see a God who pays particular, preferential attention to the vulnerable. For those who are overlooked, mistreated, taken advantage of, or simply erased from social memory, God takes up their causes. We see this through Exodus, the Levitical laws, the prophetic books, and Psalms and Proverbs, and out of this tradition, Jesus offers the gospel.

In Jesus's first sermon in Luke 4, he says that the Spirit of God is upon him to announce good news. Notably, the good news (in this portion of Scripture) is not the promise of a disembodied salvation located in heaven upon death. Jesus's gospel in Luke 4 is a very worldly one. He proclaimed, "The Spirit of the Lord is upon me, because he has anointed me to proclaim good news to the poor. He has sent me to proclaim liberty to the captives and recovering of sight to the blind, to set at liberty those who are oppressed, to proclaim the year of the Lord's favor" (verses 18–19).

This passage has often been so spiritualized that we miss the material urgency in Jesus's words and consequently the urgency and passion that will characterize Christ followers. The "poor" Jesus spoke of are certainly those who are spiritually destitute, but they are also those who are materially impoverished. The "captives" he proclaims freedom to are not just those in personal bondage to demonic powers but also those who are captive to demonic ideologies. The recovery of sight for "the blind" is not just an act of private healing but also a miracle of justice, joining the infirmed to the larger community. The "oppressed" who are set free are those who are oppressed by not only their own sin but also the sinful powers that marginalize people.

In short, we can't fully understand Jesus or his gospel without understanding justice. God in Christ—through his life, death, and resurrection—makes all things right and calls his people to follow him. How, then, do we activate this justice gene? Here are a few ways to consider.

Practicing Justice Doesn't Have to Be "Big"

We don't have to be Martin Luther King Jr. to practice justice. While every person is called to practice justice, not every person gives expression to that call in the same way. Some have been called to publicly and widely name areas of injustice and to lead the way in seeing just environments, systems, and policies come to fruition. Others might be called to support leaders or movements in more local, unseen ways. This is critically important because in the loud social media world in which we live, those who are most known and praised for practicing justice are those who are most publicly engaged. But we can all do our part.

Practicing Justice Means Being Near God and the Vulnerable

Practicing justice becomes a possibility when we are present to God and in close proximity to the vulnerable among us. To practice justice requires us to practice presence. It's important to note that Jesus lived three decades before he began his ministry. It seems that he prayerfully and patiently took the time to understand the spiritual and social landscape that surrounded him. He preached and prophesied as one who was informed. He recognized the idolatry, could name the oppression, and truly saw the people who were treated unjustly by the powers that be. More than stopping by for a photo op and short press conference after a tragedy, Jesus moved into the neighborhood. The work of deeply formed justice requires a willingness to stay present well after the adrenaline-flowing outrage has passed.

Practicing Justice Requires Us to Name Our Burdens

We must name our burdens to practice justice. In other words, the particular issues that bring about grief, anger, or compassion must be named. We all have particular parts to play in God's redemptive plan, and these parts are often discerned through the burdens we carry for a particular people, issue, or call. Novelist and theologian Frederick Buechner captured this truth well: "The place God calls you to is the place where your deep gladness and the world's deep hunger meet."[6] If I could modify that quote for the sake of this work, I'd add that God calls us to the place where our deep burdens surface.

In this world, there is a lot of injustice to go around. On a daily basis, we come across stories and experiences that provide opportunities for us to compassionately respond. Whether the injustice is related to economic, racial, gender, or environmental matters, we are all touched by different points of pain. What deeply troubles one person might not necessarily impact another. That notwithstanding, as we seek to be faithful to Jesus and his kingdom, we must name the burdens that trouble us. In the naming of our burdens, we are given the freedom to live within our limits.

We can't fix everything. Truthfully, we can't fix *most* things. But we can, by God's grace and the Spirit's empowerment, do our part to bear witness to the just and compassionate heart of God.

Practicing Justice Means Raising Our Voices

The practice of justice calls us to raise our voices. In this noisy world, raising our voices sounds like a useless enterprise. Everyone, it seems, is raising his or her voice. Social media feels like one large gathering where everyone is shouting over the next person, trying to get a message across. It is not a stretch to say we live in the most overly communicated age in history.

There's a lot of chatter in our world. In an information age, we have what political commentator and author Thomas Friedman called the "democratization of information."[7] The blessing in this is that essentially everyone has access and a platform to speak. The problem with this, as you'll likely know firsthand, is that almost everyone has access and a platform to speak. Every second, around 6,000 tweets are tweeted on Twitter, which amounts to more than 350,000 tweets sent per minute, 500 million tweets per day, and 200 billion tweets per year.[8]

Even so, justice requires us to raise our own voices. As Dr. King famously said, "A time comes when silence is betrayal."[9] A voice is one of the most powerful catalysts for justice. Whether our voices are raised through visual art, poetry, preaching, blogging, tweeting, community organizing, protesting, marching, or some other form of resistance, justice requires our voices. At the same time, how we raise our voices matters.

Practicing Justice Requires Community and Collaboration

We need community and collaboration to practice justice. As we join ourselves to others, the synergy brought about by our stories, strengths, and experiences provides an environment where greater change can take place. For those feeling their justice gene rising up, let's remember that many others have paved a way for us to walk through. As I write this, the United States has experienced yet another mass shooting. In this moment, there is a sense of despair and helplessness that has filled the minds of many. At the same time, there are leaders and organizations that have slowly and steadily worked for justice in this area, working diligently for just public policies. The practice of justice can be deepened as we support the people already in the trenches. This calls us to some form of collaboration within and beyond our local communities, with a view toward the common good of all.

Practicing Justice Means Taking Up One's Cross

We must take up our cross to practice justice. Make no mistake about it; to address injustice is to provoke the powers. Just look at Jesus. Over the past two thousand years, theologians have written countless pages exploring why Jesus died on a cross. There is not one reason alone that explains why Jesus died, but one reason that often goes overlooked is his commitment to justice. His acts of healing were not tent-revival miracles; they were acts of social subversion.

Jesus repeatedly reimagined what it meant to fulfill the law, and in his radical teaching and actions, he was consistently seen as a threat to the existing order. Jesus was killed for many reasons, but chief was his work for justice. And throughout history, he was not alone. The work for justice is dangerous. In the questioning of the status quo, the exposing of the fears and idols of others, and the naming of our complicity, we subject ourselves to pain. The suffering that comes our way might come in the form of losing friendships, experiencing family estrangement, or being subject to blackballing, bullying, physical threats, or church excommunication. Striving for justice is not for the faint of heart, yet this is the deeply formed way of Jesus.

THE PRACTICE OF COMMISSIONING IN OUR WORK

One of the sayings in our church is that everyone is called to full-time ministry. Every twelve to eighteen months, we have a Sunday commissioning service. The purpose of the service is not to commission people to different parts of the world as missionaries (a beautiful act, of course) but to commission people to their places of work in service of the gospel and the common good. The workplaces we find ourselves in offer us incalculable opportunities to practice missional presence. Before I go into a few practical ways to live into this, let me offer a brief theological overview of the nature of work and its relation to mission.

The Workplace and Our Spiritual Formation

There's something many of us wrestle with called the Sunday-night blues. Friday sets off the weekend with joy and relaxation. That joy and relaxation fills our Saturdays and our Sunday mornings and afternoons, but something happens at 6:00 p.m. on Sunday. Whatever joy we had turns into dread, and whatever relaxation we had turns into resentment, because in just a few hours we have to go back to work.

Nevertheless, the workplace is a primary place (arguably *the* primary place) for spiritual growth. Whether your work is as a teacher, lawyer, police officer, accountant, or stay-at-home parent, it's an opportunity for spiritual formation. One practical reason for this is that we will spend a significant amount of time in the workplace, surrounded by many different kinds of people. In a given lifetime, the average American will spend more than one hundred thousand hours at the workplace.[10]

The workplace is a primary place (arguably *the* primary place) for spiritual growth.

When you factor in the long commutes in traffic or train delays, we spend a lot of time in work-related activity (never mind the unpaid work we all have to do).

The workplace is often where our identities are shaped. One of the first questions we ask people when we meet them is, "So, what do you do?" For many, what you do is an expression of who you are. Spiritually speaking, this is a dangerous approach because our identities are rooted in something that can't give us what only God can. Yet for the growth of our spiritual lives, work and the workplace are critical components of a deeply formed mission. We see this from the onset of Scripture.

In Genesis 1, all it takes is five words into the Bible to depict God as a worker: "In the beginning, God *created*" (emphasis added). God is seen as one who is actively on mission. God is not up in heaven enjoying grapes while angelic beings fan with their wings. No, this God is creating, hovering, speaking, and getting his hands dirty. Likewise, the Son of God himself works. Jesus didn't spend the majority of his life as some detached spiritualist, too good for work; he spent most of his life as a carpenter, working with his hands.

Seeing All Work as Holy

This simple theological conviction that all work is holy is a necessary correction to a worldview that splits work into two categories: sacred and secular. According to many, the "holy" work is supposed to be exclusively that which relates to God, the church, missions, or humanitarian endeavors. And, of course, this work is holy. But it's not the only holy work. The work of artists, builders, teachers, parents, entrepreneurs, and bus drivers is on the same level. We collectively join to make the world a better place, each of us doing our part. To see all work as holy is a spiritual practice that pushes back on a spiritual elitism that obscures God's good vision for all creation.

Working as unto the Lord

In the book of Colossians, Paul began by noting that Jesus has supremacy over all things and that, therefore, all of life matters. But later in the epistle, Paul got word that some Christians had not been working with that in mind. There was a disconnection between their worship and their work. They worked one way when the boss was around and another when the boss was out (something we are all familiar with). In the third chapter, Paul made it plain. He wrote that believers should be motivated to work well for their bosses "not only when their eye is on you and to curry their favor" (verse 22, NIV). He then said, "It is the Lord Christ you are serving" (verse 24, NIV). This statement serves as the ultimate foundation for our work—namely, that we are working for Jesus.

When we have our commissioning services at New Life, we try to drive this home. Toward the end of the service, we acknowledge people in the various professions they give themselves to. In the process, we remind them that their work is done as an expression of worship to God. Then we say, if you're an accountant, you count your numbers with care as if you're doing Jesus's bookkeeping. If you're a car salesperson, you sell that car as if you're selling it to Christ. For computer programmers, it is Jesus's computer you are working on; construction managers, it's Jesus's house you are building; sanitation workers, you pick up all the garbage that fell out of the can because it's Jesus's street you're cleaning; educators, Jesus is one of your students. Musicians play or create to bring Christ joy. And hairdressers—it's Jesus's hair you're cutting. The list goes on. We work for Christ.

Offering High-Quality Work

It's often the case that when we go to work, we think our first task is to evangelize everyone (like I tried to do in the story from the previous chapter). We want to believe that God has sent us there to convert people. When this becomes our priority, the quality of our work is often an afterthought. We are there, certainly, to be the presence of Jesus, but we are to express his presence primarily through our good work.

I'm reminded of the words of poet and essayist Dorothy Sayers, who wrote that "the very first demand that [a carpenter's] religion makes upon him is that he should make good tables."[11] What good is our witness to Christ if we talk about him to everyone but do our jobs poorly? This is why offering high-quality work is part of our missional call. When I speak of our work being of this quality, I have in mind integrity of character as well as our commitment to demonstrating excellence. In the words of Dr. King, "If it falls your lot to be a street sweeper, sweep streets like Michelangelo painted pictures, like Shakespeare wrote poetry, like Beethoven composed music; sweep streets so well that all the host of Heaven and earth will have to pause to say, 'Here lived a great street sweeper, who swept his job well.' "[12]

To live in this way takes much effort and a deep recognition of God's presence at the workplace. Like many people, I've had jobs that I couldn't stand. One of my first jobs out of college was a four-month temporary assignment in which I had to remove staples from stacks of paper and sort the pages. Every. Single. Day. To say it was terrible is an understatement. There are some jobs and professions that make it difficult to offer high-quality work. But if we will remember that part of our work is the spirit in which we do it, God will work through our lives.

Deeply formed mission resists the pull of compartmentalization. We don't bring just our skills and aptitude to the workplace; we bring our very selves. Our being is connected to our doing. We don't work merely to be productive. Our presence is a valuable gift we bring to the ethos of the workplace. That is why we can't separate monastic rhythms from the work we do. Unless we carve out periods to stop and be with God, we can get swept away by the pressures and demands of a society that places ultimate value on the bottom line.

There's a friend of mine named Luke who works as an air-traffic controller. After I gave a sermon series on faith and work, he emailed me to share some of the ways he tries to offer high-quality work:

> Because I'm an air-traffic controller, the sermon series on work has just encouraged me to be a quiet, calm, humble, self-controlled presence in a very loud, aggressive, panic-stricken, four-letter-every-other-word, high-stress environment. It's actually very easy to be a witness on the job: you just refrain from cursing for about fifteen minutes and people wonder what your problem is. It is slowly becoming a labor of love to organize and sequence massive airplanes hurling at each other at four hundred miles per hour, and when I'm conscious of the Holy Spirit, the stress seems to lift, almost as if the Lord were guiding the airplanes through the tangled web of the New York/New Jersey airspace.

Identity Is Not Our Work

There are two ways of thinking about work that keep us from embodying it as a missional practice: we demonize it or we divinize it.

We demonize work when we do it as a necessary evil. Work becomes something we must do so we can do what we want on the weekends. I work to pay bills. I work to eat. Work is an obstacle, it's a drag, it's boring, it's demon possessed, and we hate it. It's not usually seen as an extension of our worship; rather, it's seen as an experience of warfare.

There are two ways of thinking about work that keep us from embodying it as a missional practice: we demonize it or we divinize it.

We can also divinize work. In this way of thinking, work is elevated to a godlike status. Work becomes a necessary means of securing our identities. For some of us, our work is our primary means of our identities, which is why unemployment and retirement reveal much about the states of our souls. We end up pouring so much into our work that it becomes the only way we understand ourselves.

Divinization of our work is when our salary becomes our god, our position represents our significance, and our success and ability to climb the ladder make us feel important. But for the deeply formed persons on mission, our work is something we are called to steward life with, not suck life from. Our sense of meaning is found in the love of God, not in what we produce with our hands. This is why Sabbath keeping is an indispensable practice. As we rest, we announce to ourselves and the world that our identities come from a different place.

THE PRACTICE OF ANNOUNCING THE GOSPEL

The final deeply formed missional practice I want to explore is that of announcing the gospel. Although this might sound like a practice exclusively undertaken by pastors and evangelists, this is part and parcel of what it means for every follower of Jesus to be deeply formed.

When I became a Christian, the announcing of the gospel was relegated to church services and street preaching. I initially believed that my job was to speak the truth of God widely and publicly, washing my hands of any guilt in the event that people didn't believe the good news. The rationale was, "I've done my job here. The rest is up to you." This version of announcing the gospel leaves much to be desired. First off, it misses the particular ways God wants good news to come to people inundated by bad news. Second, it often locates good news through a moralistic framework. Third, it eliminates the up-close experience God desires we have with people. To announce the gospel is not just for the large Christian gathering; it's for the encounters we have with people on a day-to-day basis.

As I wrote earlier, the essence of the gospel is the lordship of Jesus Christ. In his life, atoning death, resurrection, and ascension, Jesus has redeemed (and is redeeming) the world. The good news, simply stated, is the recognition that Jesus is Lord over all things and invites us to a life free from the shackles of bondage. This Jesus also calls us to join him (in the power of his Spirit) in being a liberating presence to the world around us. One of the ways we join him is in announcing the gospel. I submit that it requires a posture of openness, whereby we refuse to generically impose formulaic steps that don't compassionately consider the particular blockages that keep people from relationship with God.

In my early years as a Christian, I was taught various models of evangelism. The models are often rooted in solid biblical truth, but the attempt to scale and make evangelism accessible to everyone turns the announcing of the gospel into a stale and transaction-oriented encounter. This approach also keeps us in control, bringing our rehearsed solution to a problem we know little about. But the announcing of the gospel is a practice that requires careful discernment, compassionate curiosity, and a willingness to step beyond a transaction of faith.

In his book *Faithful Presence*, David Fitch wrote about preaching the gospel. He made a particularly salient point about control:

> Proclaiming the gospel is a profoundly decentering experience that places the hearer in submission to God. It is the opposite of being in control. Proclaiming the gospel starts with, "Are you hopeless? Are you caught in a world gone wrong? Have you become caught up in sin? Are you powerless? Are you being destroyed by the world, by injustice? The gospel is that God has come in Jesus Christ and defeated the powers. God has made Jesus Lord. He therefore rules and is working in all of your circumstances, personal and in the world. Will you give up control, submit to Jesus as Lord, and participate in this new world?"[13]

The questions that Fitch laid out are not to be used as a template per se, but they offer a different starting point for announcing the gospel. The truth is, every person we come into contact with has experienced, is experiencing, or will experience significant pain. Every person will eventually feel stuck and long to escape. Every person, at some point, will undergo a powerlessness that leads to despair. As we offer our presence, lovingly and patiently listening to others, we will find ourselves in a better space to noncoercively offer words of hope, announcing that Christ is present and worthy of trust.

To announce the gospel in a deeply formed way moves us beyond techniques and one-size-fits-all strategies. As Jesus perfectly modeled, we are called to open ourselves to joining the journeys of others, building relationship, discerning openness, and announcing the news of God's loving presence and commitment toward them. This is not cookie-cutter evangelism, and we will find ourselves unsure of how to move forward. But this is the nature of faith, isn't it?

AFTERWORD:
THE DEEPLY FORMED WAY FORWARD

A young German pastor writing from prison and nearing the end of his life asked a simple question that countless people have returned to. In his correspondence with his friends, he had been wrestling with many issues pertaining to the nature of religion, the rapidly changing world, and the witness of the church in a time when Adolf Hitler was destroying countless lives. With penetrating force, this young pastor stated, "What is bothering me incessantly is the question what Christianity really is, or indeed who Christ really is, for us today." This prophetic question was asked by German evangelical pastor Dietrich Bonhoeffer in 1944.[1]

Today we must ask an equally incisive question: Who are *we*, really, for Christ today? Both questions call us to seriously consider our lives. And honestly, the current state of things is not encouraging. We find ourselves in a world increasingly shaped by dangerous rhythms, racial hostility, emotional immaturity, flippant sexuality, political idolatry, and individualistic consumerism, to name a few of the powers wreaking havoc in our lives and communities. We must ask:

- How can it be that those who call themselves Christians live at such a destructive pace that eliminates any semblance of abiding with Jesus in prayer?

- How can it be that those who identify as followers of Christ still hold deeply racist beliefs about others?

- How can it be that those who consider themselves disciples of Jesus live lives characterized by emotional dysfunction?

- How can it be that those who believe that God became a human lack serious integration when it comes to our bodies and our spirituality?

- How is it that those called to be the very presence of Jesus in the world live indistinguishably from the world?

These questions are a clarion call reminding us that it is certainly possible to be deeply committed to identifying with the external trappings of Christianity while still living lives that are radically incongruent with life in the kingdom. They tell us that it is certainly possible to be deeply committed to identifying with a shallow form of Christianity but not be deeply formed by Christ.

I don't believe that God is interested in transforming some parts of us and leaving the rest untouched. Scripture does not show him calling us to split life into sacred and nonsacred categories. When I reflect on the New Testament, I see how Jesus has redeemed the entire world and calls our lives to reflect this good news by seeing God shape every aspect of our lives.

The best witness we have is our transformed lives.

So to come full circle, when I speak of being deeply formed, I'm specifically referring to a way of being in the world that's marked by new rhythms, contemplative presence, and interior awareness, which results in lives that work for reconciliation, justice, and peace while seeing the sacredness of all of life. It is this kind of life that God wants to form in us. Why? Because our transformation in all these areas is one of the most effective ways to see a world come to experience God's saving love.

The best witness we have as the church is not our good music, nor the programs that meet felt needs, nor the quality of the edifice that people worship in. The best witness we have is our transformed lives. So how do we bring together all that we've learned? I believe we need a rule.

A DEEPLY FORMED RULE OF LIFE

A rule of life is a way of intentionally ordering our everyday so that we love God and others and see every component of our lives as holy. This *rule* doesn't mean a list of rules. It's more of a set of practices, relationships, and commitments that is inspired by the Spirit for the sake of our wholeness in Christ.

I recognize that in this book, I somewhat formidably offered plenty of practices for you to consider. By no means are we expected to master them all. The purpose of the practices is not to put them on a checklist, do them, and move on. My hope is that you would be attentive to the particular practices that you need in a given season in your life. For instance, if you are in a season in which you are trying to make sense of the racial complexity of our world, the practices related by reconciliation are what you might need right then. Or if you are looking for healing in an area of sexuality, the practices found in the chapters on sexual wholeness might be what you should focus on.

An easy way to take the next step is to create a deeply formed rule for yourself. List one or two practices from each of the five I covered: contemplative rhythms, racial reconciliation, interior examination, sexual wholeness, and missional presence. To identify the practices you need most, consider such questions as:

- Where do I sense most stress happening in my life?

- What practices is this season calling me to engage in?

- Where do I have significant gaps?

- Where am I called to lead others?

- Which practices might help me to help others?

These questions can bring clarity to how God is leading you. After you identify the practices, invite a friend or small group to join you in exploring them. It's often in the context of relationships and conversation that we find deeper layers of truth. The practices are our lifelong companions because we are on a never-ending journey of being formed.

THE FUTURE OF CHRISTIANITY

As I think about the future of Christianity in our world, I'm convinced that followers of Jesus have a great opportunity before us. The way of the world continues to swallow people in its pace, hostility, distractions, and shallowness.

Having the right answers to the questions of faith is helpful but will not do much to form people in the way of Jesus. We need more than answers found in arguments. We need answers found in our very lives. We need to locate integrative answers to the fundamental questions that reside not only in the head but in the entire person.

When we take seriously the task to follow Jesus and reflect his transforming power in all aspects of life, we will be at a place where the claims of the gospel take root in deeper ways. To this end, may we work in the power of God's Spirit to see Christ formed in our lives, our churches, and the world.

ACKNOWLEDGMENTS

I'm profoundly indebted to a community of people who have helped me bring this book to life. When eyes other than mine began to read some of my early drafts, I realized how many blind spots I had, as well as the communal nature of writing. It takes a village to write a book.

Many thanks goes to my agent, Alex Field. You have consistently been a presence of encouragement. Thank you to my editor, Shannon Marchese, for your guidance. Your insights were invaluable. I couldn't have picked a better editor for my first book.

Thank you to Joseph Terry, Tommy Ortiz, Phil Varghese, Glenn Packiam, Dante Stewart, Jose Humphreys, and Kristian Hernandez. Your feedback on various chapters affirmed and clarified much of this book. Special thanks to Arnaldo Santiago Jr., who read every word and gently offered brilliant perspectives that only enhanced this book.

I would like to thank my church family, New Life Fellowship, where I have been a pastor for twelve years and served as lead pastor for the past seven of those. I could not have asked for a better community to lead. Your generosity knows no bounds. It's a privilege to serve you. Incalculable thanks to our staff. Every week, I have the joy of leading alongside you. Your encouragement, feedback, and playfulness have been pure grace. Sincere thanks also to our board of elders. Thank you for helping me discern the timing of this project and for releasing me to serve our local congregation and beyond through this book.

My life, marriage, and leadership are impossible to understand without the influence of Pete and Geri Scazzero. Thank you both for modeling a deeply formed life and for entrusting me with the once-in-a-lifetime opportunity to water the seeds you planted more than three decades ago at New Life Fellowship.

Thank you to my siblings, Jason, Laura, and Michelle. And special thanks to my sister, Melissa, for graciously reading everything I sent your way. All of you have enriched my life beyond calculation.

To my mother, Nicolasa, and my father, Richard Sr., thank you. Your tireless love and affirmation have been a source of strength all my life. I love you.

Thank you to Karis and Nathan, my children. The joy you have given me as your father can never be fully expressed. You have both taught me many lessons. Daddy loves you.

And finally, to Rosie, my beloved wife. This book would not have been written without you. Many years ago, you believed in me as a writer and called out my gifts. Thank you for being my best friend. Your love has deeply formed me.

NOTES

INTRODUCTION: FORMED BY A SHALLOW WORLD

1. Leonard Klady, " 'Titanic' Sails to All-Time Box-Office Record," *Variety,* March 3, 1998, https://variety.com/1998/film/news/titanic-sails-to-all-time-box-office-record-1201345048/.

2. Navigation Center, "How Much of an Iceberg Is Below the Water," United States Coast Guard, www.navcen.uscg.gov/?pageName=iipHowMuchOfAnIcebergIsBelowTheWater.

CHAPTER 1: CONTEMPLATIVE RHYTHMS FOR AN EXHAUSTED LIFE

1. John H. Girdner, *Newyorkitis* (New York: Grafton, 1901), 27.

2. Parker J. Palmer, *Let Your Life Speak: Listening for the Voice of Vocation* (San Francisco: Jossey-Bass, 2000), 49.

3. Kosuke Koyama, *Three-Mile-an-Hour God* (United Kingdom: SCM Press, 2015).

4. N. T. Wright. *GodSpeed, The Pace of Being Known,* documentary film, 36:53, www.livegodspeed.org/watchgodspeed.

5. Dallas Willard, quoted in John Ortberg, *Soul Keeping: Caring for the Most Important Part of You* (Grand Rapids, MI: Zondervan, 2014), 20.

6. Ken Shigematsu, *God in My Everything: How an Ancient Rhythm Helps Busy People Enjoy God* (Grand Rapids, MI: Zondervan, 2013), 20.

7. Justo L. González, *The Story of Christianity*, vol. 1, *The Early Church to the Dawn of the Reformation*, rev. ed. (New York: Harper Collins, 2010), 125–26.

8. González, *Story of Christianity*, 157.

9. Thomas Merton, *Conjectures of a Guilty Bystander* (New York: Doubleday, 1966), 92.

CHAPTER 2: DEEPLY FORMED
PRACTICES OF CONTEMPLATIVE RHYTHMS

1. Robert Cardinal Sarah, *The Power of Silence: Against the Dictatorship of Noise* (San Francisco: Ignatius Press, 2017), 27–28.

2. Marjorie J. Thompson, *The Gift of Encouragement: Restoring Heart to Those Who Have Lost It* (Nashville: Abingdon, 2013), 92–93.

3. Lily Kuo and Quartz, "Japan May Force Its Workers to Take Vacation," *Atlantic*, February 5, 2015, theatlantic.com /international/archive/2015/02/japan-may-force-its-workers -to-take-vacation/385210.

4. Eugene H. Peterson, *Eat This Book: A Conversation in the Art of Spiritual Reading* (Grand Rapids, MI: Eerdmans, 2006), 2.

CHAPTER 3: RACIAL
RECONCILIATION FOR A DIVIDED WORLD

1. Peter Scazzero, *The Emotionally Healthy Church: A Strategy for Discipleship That Actually Changes Lives* (Grand Rapids, MI: Zondervan, 2015) and *Emotionally Healthy Spirituality: It's Impossible to Be Spiritually Mature While Remaining Emotionally Immature* (Grand Rapids, MI: Zondervan, 2017).

2. I should note that when we talk about reconciliation at New Life, we address it from five perspectives: racial, ethnic, economic, gender, and generational. For our purposes in this chapter, I will emphasize the racial and ethnic perspectives.

3. George Eldon Ladd, *The Gospel of the Kingdom: Scriptural Studies in the Kingdom of God* (Grand Rapids, MI: Eerdmans, 1990), 16.

4. Jessica Liber, "The Filter Bubble Is Your Own Damn Fault, Says Facebook," *Fast Company,* May 7, 2015, www.fastcompany .com/3046032/the-filter-bubble-is-your-own-damn-fault-says -facebook.

5. Brenda Salter McNeil, *Roadmap to Reconciliation: Moving Communities into Unity, Wholeness, and Justice* (Downers Grove, IL: InterVarsity, 2015), 22.

6. Lisa Sharon Harper, *The Very Good Gospel: How Everything Wrong Can Be Made Right* (Colorado Springs, CO: WaterBrook, 2016), 140, 146.

7. James Baldwin, GoodReads.com, www.goodreads.com /quotes/14374-not-everything-that-is-faced-can-be-changed -but-nothing.

8. Michael O. Emerson, *The Persistent Problem* (Waco: TX: Center for Christian Ethics at Baylor University, 2010), www .baylor.edu/content/services/document.php/110974.pdf.

9. Cornel West, GoodReads.com, www.goodreads.com/author /quotes/6176.Cornel_West.

10. Michael O. Emerson and Christian Smith, *Divided by Faith: Evangelical Religion and the Problem of Faith in America* (New York: Oxford University Press, 2000).

CHAPTER 4: DEEPLY FORMED
PRACTICES OF RACIAL RECONCILIATION

1. Eddie S. Glaude Jr., *Democracy in Black: How Race Still Enslaves the American Soul* (New York: Crown, 2017), 55, 56.

2. James Baldwin, *Nobody Knows My Name* (New York: Vintage, 1992), 61.

3. Bryan Stevenson, "Opinion: This Is the Conversation About Race That We Need to Have Now," Ideas.Ted.Com, August 17, 2017, https://ideas.ted.com/opinion-this-is-the-conversation -about-race-that-we-need-to-have-now.

4. George Yancy, "Dear White America," *New York Times,* December 24, 2015, https://opinionator.blogs.nytimes.com /2015/12/24/dear-white-america.

5. Peter Scazzero, *The Emotionally Healthy Church: A Strategy for Discipleship That Actually Changes Lives* (Grand Rapids, MI: Zondervan, 2015), chapter 10.

6. *Munyurangabo,* directed by Isaac Lee Chung (Brooklyn, NY: Almond Tree Films, 2007), DVD.

7. Personal email to the author from Isaac Lee Chung on October 17, 2013.

8. Soong-Chan Rah, *Prophetic Lament: A Call for Justice in Troubled Times* (Downers Grove, IL: InterVarsity, 2015), 23.

9. Parker J. Palmer, *Let Your Life Speak: Listening for the Voice of Vocation* (San Francisco: Jossey-Bass, 1999), chapter 5.

10. Coretta Scott King, quoted in The Schomburg Center for Research in Black Culture, *Standing in the Need of Prayer: A Celebration of Black Prayer* (New York: Free Press, 2003), x.

11. Walter Brueggemann, *The Prophetic Imagination* (Minneapolis: Fortress, 1978).

12. Willie James Jennings, *The Christian Imagination: Theology and the Origins of Race* (New Haven, CT: Yale University, 2010), 59.

13. Alastair Bonnett, quoted in Daniel Hill, *White Awake: An Honest Look at What It Means to Be White* (Downers Grove, IL: 2017), 31.

14. *The Book of Common Prayer and Administration of the Sacraments and Other Rites and Ceremonies of the Church* (New York: Oxford University Press, 2005), 79.

15. Miroslav Volf, *Exclusion and Embrace: A Theological Exploration of Identity, Otherness, and Reconciliation* (Nashville: Abingdon, 1996), 124.

CHAPTER 5: INTERIOR EXAMINATION
FOR A WORLD LIVING ON THE SURFACE

1. Alice Miller, *The Body Never Lies: The Lingering Effects of Hurtful Parenting,* trans. Andrew Jenkins (New York: Norton, 2005), 119.

2. Ronald Rolheiser, *The Holy Longing: The Search for a Christian Spirituality* (New York: Crown, 2014), 32.

3. "Check Yo Self," MP3 audio, track 13 on Ice Cube, *The Predator,* Priority, 1992.

4. John Calvin, *Institutes of the Christian Religion* (Grand Rapids, MI: Eerdmans, 1957), 1:37.

5. Richard Rohr and Andreas Ebert, *The Enneagram: A Christian Perspective* (Claudius Verlag, Munich: Crossroad, 1999), xi.

6. Parker J. Palmer, *On the Brink of Everything: Grace, Gravity, and Getting Old* (San Francisco: Berrett-Koehler, 2018), 146.

7. David Benner, *The Gift of Being Yourself: The Sacred Call to Self-Discovery* (Downers Grove, IL: InterVarsity, 2015), 50.

8. Benner, *Gift of Being Yourself,* 51.

CHAPTER 6: DEEPLY FORMED PRACTICES OF INTERIOR EXAMINATION

1. Donald Winnicott, quoted in Lesley Caldwell and Angela Joyce, *Reading Winnicott* (New York: Routledge, 2011), 206.

2. Robert Stolorow, *Trauma and Human Existence: Autobiographical, Psychoanalytic, and Philosophical Reflections* (New York: Routledge, 2007), 10.

3. Pastor Pete Scazzero's book *The Emotionally Healthy Church* provides a helpful theological overview of genograms and offers additional ways forward.

4. Peter L. Steinke, *Congregational Leadership in Anxious Times: Being Calm and Courageous No Matter What* (Lanham, MD: Rowman and Littlefield, 2006), 10.

5. Alice Miller, *The Body Never Lies: The Lingering Effects of Hurtful Parenting,* trans. Andrew Jenkins (New York: Norton, 2005), 14.

6. Peter Scazzero and Geri Scazzero, *Emotionally Healthy Relationships Workbook* (Grand Rapids, MI: Zondervan, 2017), 82.

CHAPTER 7: SEXUAL WHOLENESS FOR A CULTURE THAT SPLITS BODIES FROM SOULS

1. Alan Leeds, quoted in Touré, "Prince's Holy Lust," *New York Times,* April 22, 2016, www.nytimes.com/2016/04/24/opinion/sunday/princes-holy-lust.html.

2. Ronald Rolheiser, *The Holy Longing: The Search for a Christian Spirituality* (New York: Crown, 2014), 34.

3. Debra Hirsch, *Redeeming Sex: Naked Conversations About Sexuality and Spirituality* (Downers Grove, IL: InterVarsity, 2015), 26.

4. Marva Dawn, *Sexual Character: Beyond Technique to Intimacy* (Grand Rapids, MI: Eerdmans, 1993), 10.

5. Dawn, *Sexual Character,* 10.

6. Dawn, *Sexual Character,* 10.

7. Dawn, *Sexual Character,* 12.

8. Christopher West, *Fill These Hearts: God, Sex, and the Universal Longing* (New York: Image, 2018).

9. Shaji George Kochuthara, *The Concept of Sexual Pleasure in the Catholic Moral Tradition* (Rome: Gregorian University Press, 2007), 148–49.

10. Peter Brown, *The Body and Society: Men, Women, and Sexual Renunciation in Early Christianity* (New York: Columbia University, 2008), 173.

11. Saint Augustine, *Confessions,* trans. Sarah Ruden (New York: Modern Library, 2018), 223.

12. C. S. Lewis, *Mere Christianity* (New York: HarperOne, 2015), 136–37.

CHAPTER 8: DEEPLY FORMED PRACTICES OF SEXUAL WHOLENESS

1. Dallas Willard, quoted in Mike Sullivan, "The Divine Conspiracy: The Grandest Prayer of All Is the Lord's Prayer by Dallas Willard," *Emmaus City* (blog), May 24, 2018, http://

emmauscity.blogspot.com/2018/05/the-divine-conspiracy
-rediscovering-our.html.

2. "May Launches Government's First Loneliness Strategy,"
Government Business, October 15, 2018, https://
governmentbusiness.co.uk/news/15102018/may-launches
-government%e2%80%99s-first-loneliness-strategy.

3. Personal email to the author from Sue on October 31,
2013.

4. Bessel van der Kolk, *The Body Keeps the Score: Brain, Mind,
and Body in the Healing of Trauma* (New York: Penguin
Random House, 2014), 125–26.

5. Richard Wagamese, *Embers: One Ojibway's Meditations*
(Madeira Park, BC: Douglas and McIntyre, 2017), 55.

CHAPTER 9: MISSIONAL PRESENCE
IN A DISTRACTED AND DISENGAGED WORLD

1. Thomas Merton, *The Seven Storey Mountain: An Autobiography
of Faith* (New York: Harcourt Brace Jovanovich, 1948), 197.

2. Homer Simpson, quoted in Mostly Simpsons, "The Simpsons
Everybody's a Sinner, Except for This Guy," YouTube video, :15,
May 18, 2016, www.youtube.com/watch?v=8OPJYbgD45Q.

3. Jürgen Moltmann, *The Trinity and the Kingdom*
(Minneapolis: Fortress, 1993), 174–75.

4. Mother Teresa, GoodReads.com, www.goodreads.com
/quotes/2887-if-you-judge-people-you-have-no-time-to-love.

CHAPTER 10: DEEPLY FORMED
PRACTICES OF MISSIONAL PRESENCE

1. Kate Taylor and Jeffrey E. Singer, "In Queens, Immigrants
Clash with Residents of New Homeless Shelter," *New York Times,*
July 25, 2014, www.nytimes.com/2014/07/26/nyregion
/homeless-shelters-opening-in-queens-stirs-ugly-exchanges.html.

2. Henri J. M. Nouwen, *Reaching Out: The Three Movements of
the Spiritual Life* (New York: Image, 1986), 71.

3. Nadia Whitehead, "That's Not Fair! Crime and Punishment in a Preschooler's Mind," *NPR*, June 24, 2015, www.npr.org /sections/health-shots/2015/06/24/415495362/thats-not -fair-crime-and-punishment-in-a-preschoolers-mind.

4. Whitehead, "That's Not Fair!"

5. Timothy Keller, *Generous Justice: How God's Grace Makes Us Just* (New York: Penguin Books, 2012), 4.

6. Frederick Buechner, GoodReads.com, www.goodreads.com /quotes/140448-the-place-god-calls-you-to-is-the-place-where.

7. Thomas L. Friedman, *The Lexus and the Olive Tree: Understanding Globalization* (New York: Farrar, Straus & Giroux, 2000), 66.

8. David Sayce, "The Number of Tweets Per Day in 2019," www.dsayce.com/social-media/tweets-day.

9. Martin Luther King Jr., "Beyond Vietnam: A Time to Break Silence" (speech, April 4, 1967, Riverside Church), audio, 1:55:40, https://soundcloud.com/kinginstitute/vietnam-a -crisis-of-conscience.

10. Leigh Campbell, "We've Broken Down Your Entire Life into Years Spent Doing Tasks," *Huffington Post Australia*, October 19, 2017, www.huffingtonpost.com.au/2017/10/18/weve-broken -down-your-entire-life-into-years-spent-doing-tasks_a_23248153.

11. Dorothy Sayers, "Why Work?," Center for Faith and Work at LeTourneau University, https://centerforfaithandwork.com /article/why-work-dorothy-sayers.

12. Martin Luther King Jr., *The Papers of Martin Luther King Jr.*, vol. 3, *Birth of a New Age, December 1955–December 1956*, ed. Clayborne Carson et al. (Berkeley, CA: University of California, 1997), 457.

13. David E. Fitch, *Faithful Presence: Seven Disciplines That Shape the Church for Mission* (Downers Grove, IL: InterVarsity, 2016), 101.

AFTERWORD: THE DEEPLY FORMED WAY FORWARD

1. Dietrich Bonhoeffer, *Letters and Papers from Prison* (New York: Simon & Schuster, 2001), 279.

ABOUT THE AUTHOR

Rich Villodas is the Brooklyn-born lead pastor of New Life Fellowship, a large multiracial church with more than seventy-five countries represented, in Elmhurst, Queens. Rich graduated with a bachelor of arts in pastoral ministry and theology from Nyack College. He went on to complete his master of divinity from Alliance Theological Seminary. He enjoys reading widely and preaching and writing on contemplative spirituality, justice-related issues, and the art of preaching. He's been married to Rosie since 2006, and they have two beautiful children, Karis and Nathan.

ABOUT THE TYPE

This book was set in Galliard, a typeface designed in 1978 by Matthew Carter (b. 1937) for the Mergenthaler Linotype Company. Galliard is based on the sixteenth-century typefaces of Robert Granjon (1513–89).